MONEY
MANAGEMENT
MINDSET

**A GUIDE TO HELP YOU PREPARE FOR
THE EXPECTED AND UNEXPECTED**

DENNIS BIELIK, CFA, CFP, FRM

RIVER GROVE
BOOKS

Published by River Grove Books
Austin, TX
www.rivergrovebooks.com

Distributed by River Grove Books

Design and composition by Greenleaf Book Group and Kim Lance
Cover design by Greenleaf Book Group and Kim Lance
Cover and interior images used under license from ©Shutterstock.com/Grey ibex
Figure on page 36 republished with permission from JPMorgan Chase & Co. (c) 2020

Publisher's Cataloging-in-Publication data is available.

Paperback ISBN: 978-1-63299-273-4

Hardcover ISBN: 978-1-63299-275-8

eBook ISBN: 978-1-63299-274-1

First Edition

"A goal without a plan is just a wish."

—ANTOINE DE SAINT-EXUPÉRY

.

CONTENTS

CONCLUSION. LIVE YOUR PLAN! 151

FOREWORD

One of my favorite axioms about life is "to expect the unexpected." This is especially true when it comes to the financial aspects of our lives. Think of it—there are more 24-hour-a-day financial and investment channels than there are for health and wellness, and yet many of us don't give our finances, and our future, the true attention they deserve. And even when we do, it can be a daunting and confusing landscape.

The journey you are about to embark on with this book is a unique assessment of the checkpoints of life and how to plan for them—and perhaps more importantly, how to enjoy them and benefit from them. Several years ago, I had the pleasure of becoming a partner with Dennis Bielik in a growing financial services business. Over the last few years, Dennis has shared an approach with me that he developed to effectively get at the deepest goals and needs of his clients. For Dennis, managing money and investing was just one tool in the overall process of enriching clients beyond just manufacturing more wealth for them. At its base level, this book is about creating peace and certainty in the future.

Successful people—in life and in business—generally do a good job of deconstructing their problems in the great quest to find solutions. Stated differently, successful and happy people are good at building paths to their goals and destinations. This book gets to the heart of that process by providing a model we can all use to understand our financial priorities and generate truly successful outcomes.

This book will be your guide for the financial journey of life. As you embark upon this worthwhile journey with Dennis, I urge you to ask yourself three key questions: If you could change anything about your current financial situation, what would it be? Second, what goals mean the most to you as you look at the next 5, 10, and 20 years of your life? And last, what solutions can you put in place now for the inevitable—the unexpected events or special challenges of life?

In these pages, you will find simple, straightforward assessments and actionable tactics to address the complex world of financial planning, investments, and wealth management. You will gain understanding regarding the major items that control our financial futures, such as budgeting, so that you gain more control over the outcomes that life will bring you and your family.

We know two things for sure about life. First, we know it would be great to go back and live like a child again—dreaming, experiencing unrestricted joy, and discovering new things every day. Most of us lose sight of that path as the years go by. Second, it would be wonderful if we also felt a sense of connection to something greater than ourselves, such as our community or spirituality, or a deeper alignment with what we love and those we love. Dennis's book provides a true model for that which we can all relate to. If you are more financially successful, you will have more ability to impact your community and your own life and the lives of those you love. In these pages, we also see that the majority of us need help—we all need someone who can be a listener, a sounding board, a problem solver, and an expert advisor. The best financial planners, who are truly life guides, can provide this type of advocacy.

If you could read a book that would make your life better, would you? This book focuses on what really builds financial success as few have done before. It has been said that "money isn't everything, but it does make everything easier." This book marries concepts of growing and protecting wealth with the basic threads that are part of the fabric of daily life, while pursuing a simple goal: Make life easier and more enjoyable.

Success is defined in as many ways as there are people in the world. Some people focus on money first. Some focus on fulfillment. Some don't focus at all. As you turn these pages, you'll find a true process for making your life journey a better one. You'll boil down the things that really make your finances tick into common-sense actionable elements.

A poignant part of why Dennis put his heart and soul into this book is his discovery after more than a decade of serving clients that so many of those people are not on the right track. Dennis was determined to create a system—a framework—that could be put into action to create better outcomes. He accomplished building a worthy outline for professional planners to follow. But more, the process herein is designed for individuals to use in coordination with their chosen personal advisors.

So go now, and enjoy the journey!

—JEFF MONTGOMERY, JD, President,
TCG Group Holdings,
Former CEO, NFP Securities

PART 1

GETTING
STARTED

INTRODUCTION

Have you ever played the board game Life? As a player, you spin a wheel with numbers 1 through 10. The spinner determines how fast or slow you move through spaces that name common life activities—college, jobs, marriage, and children, for example. You may move quickly or slowly to the finish line, depending on where the spinner lands. When it comes to a first job, your salary is determined by choosing a card at random. Throughout the game, you can pick the type of house you want to buy, or you might land on a space with an unexpected event, good or bad. Unlike in real life, you encounter these occurrences in a set order, and you have no control over them. Some spaces benefit your life, while others set you back.

Like any board game, there are winners and losers. (You probably won't win the first time you play.) But the great thing about it is that you can play more than once. You learn to strategize and improve your chances to win. Real life, of course, gives you only one chance. But we make our own choices about most of these events: Do we go to college? What type of career do we pursue? Do we get married, and do we have children? What kind of house do we purchase, or do we live in an apartment? Our decisions are important and can affect us throughout our lives.

Even more significantly, we can create a financial strategy that will help us manage not only expected milestones like marriage, children, and work but also those events that surprise us. We can learn ways to assess and regularly review what we need, want, and dream about so that our lives and those of our loved ones are as secure as we can make them.

That is my purpose with this book.

Helping people has long been a passion of mine, and it's the basis of my work in the financial field, where I've been able to draw on my own life experiences. I grew up with hardworking parents who had jobs outside of the home. They both traveled for work to support our family but always put us kids first. As a teenager, I began to work and used to ask my parents about finances. They never had a financial advisor and were very risk averse. I was curious about this because there were plenty of television shows and movies about financial advisors and people seeking their help.

It wasn't until I entered the financial services industry that I realized why my parents (and many other people) had never worked with anyone. They had undoubtedly heard of someone getting taken advantage of by a person claiming to be an advisor. Or perhaps they felt as though they didn't have enough money to warrant one. Those realizations struck me hard. The people who need help the most are reluctant to ask for help. It's been a passion of mine to address that paradox.

I was one of five boys, four of whom were born within seven years of each other and one of whom was adopted and raised as one of us. Our family experienced several tragic events: My oldest brother passed away, our house burned down, and one of my little brothers was diagnosed with a rare form of leukemia. It was more than you might expect in a single family, and it's hard to plan for those kinds of events. It's also difficult to think about finances when so much emotion is involved, but some sound financial advice would certainly have given my parents more peace of mind.

People always want to plan for positive goals, but in reality, a plan also needs to account for the risks associated with life. I know how hard it was to watch my parents go through these experiences. My goal is to help others plan for them.

The board game of Life is fun to play, and it can be a useful way of imagining how to navigate the choices, celebrations, disappointments, and surprises—the ups and down—we all face. In the following pages, we'll follow a more realistic journey through the real "game" of Life—no spinners or sheer luck involved.

1

EVERYONE NEEDS A PLAN

In late 2007, I was at my parents' house recovering from a severe auto accident. I had spent a week in intensive care and undergone a major surgery to address internal injuries, a concussion, and back and wrist injuries. I'd always been a planner and tried to plan for my future. I set goals for myself, from selecting my career to deciding how old I wanted to be when I married and had kids. But during those weeks of rest and healing, I came to realize life doesn't always follow your plan.

My dad, a CPA, was considering retirement, and we talked a lot about his future while I stayed with him and my mom. He worked for the federal government his whole career. The only thing keeping him from retirement was funding my younger brothers' college tuition. Luckily, my siblings were hardworking students and sped through their education. Looking ahead at retirement, my dad debated whether to keep his pension annuity or take a sizeable (and tempting) lump-sum payout.

When I looked closely at the pension, I saw it produced an 8 percent annuity. If he invested his payout in the stock market, he would need an 8 percent risk-free rate of return to provide the same benefit. My dad and I sat down to discuss this issue. He ended up taking the annuity. I asked him what made the decision so hard to figure out. He said he was more focused on having a legacy to pass down to us than securing his own financial freedom. The difficulty of this choice in the context of his values would stick with me as I became a financial advisor.

Throughout every individual's life, decisions need to be made at key moments: Take a job? Get married? Go through a divorce? Retire? I call big moments like these "checkpoints." They occur at any age and every stage in life. Though they may fall into familiar categories, the ultimate decisions about what to do are ours and ours alone. All checkpoints also can create financial stress.

Later in the book, we'll examine these checkpoints in detail. For now, it's important to understand that the way to reduce the stress of these major events is to have a plan—and to live it. Unfortunately, most people don't have a plan. If they do have one—whether they created it by themselves or with the help of a planner—they tend to ignore it.

Most of us have one major goal: happiness for ourselves and our loved ones. Beyond that, however, everyone's plan for achieving that goal will be unique—and should be. After all, your situation is undoubtedly different from mine.

Let me tell you about my plan. It's not built around retirement or buying a dream home. My plan is built around having enough money so that I can work for passion and fun. I love what I do, but losing my job and not being able to support my family is still a big fear. It's the outcome of my pillow test; in other words, it's what keeps me up at night. That's why it's an important part of my plan.

If you lie down at night and cannot sleep because you're concerned about something financial, that should be *your* priority as you create your own plan.

What exactly is a life plan? A financial plan focuses on retirement as the main objective. I use the term "life plan" to describe an evolved version of a financial plan. It should help you achieve more than just retirement. It should help you determine your insurance needs and create or amend an estate plan for your offspring and any charities. Every aspect of your life that involves money, from buying a home or car to making investments, should be addressed and adapted as goals change.

I'm not talking about "life planners," who are basically motivational speakers. They may help you set goals and improve your outlook and habits day to day. But that's different from having an overall financial plan that allows you to navigate through important periods of your life.

Often people use the term "life planning" to mean they assist clients with investment issues. For example, they'll review your estate documents and ensure they are up to date. That is certainly a step in the right direction. But it doesn't take into account the overall path of your life or plan for other decisions.

The real issue I have with many planners is they help you build a plan but don't actively help you take charge of it throughout your life. As they see it, you are still responsible for living the plan and keeping yourself accountable. It is up to you to notify them with changes. You may have no idea what those changes are or why and when they may occur or should occur. These so-called life planners haven't alerted you to checkpoints, nor have they given you the tools you need to deal with them effectively. As I said, it's no good to build a plan if you're unable to live it.

Moreover, if that plan is stagnant and doesn't change as our life changes, it inevitably will become useless. Even estimates of when we'll hit our checkpoints may change. Think of a long road trip. We can plot our journey on maps or on our phone and estimate the time it will take to arrive. Two things may happen: We'll get there earlier or we'll take longer than planned. Anything from a storm to a car wreck can slow us down. If we drive over the speed limit to get there faster, we risk getting stopped for speeding, delaying our arrival. Only rarely will we arrive at the exact time we expected to arrive. Life is the same way.

I'm not here to tell you if your decisions at different stages of your life are right or wrong. You don't get graded on your life plan. It's not a class; it's your life. The moment you view it as a pass-or-fail test, you may become impatient. It may become less important to you, or you may make excuses for why you are behind. A plan is an adaptive and iterative process. You need to embrace it as such. That will allow you to change the plan when you fall behind or adjust it if you are ahead of where you thought you might be.

Think back to my parents' situation. When our house burned down due to a freak accident, it set them back, but there was no point in giving up. It meant they had to adapt to get back on track for their goals. (Luckily, my parents had insurance that covered the fire. Everyone should have home or rental insurance.)

Creating a life plan is not a simple task. You can't look at a board game and trust that college, marriage, children, or jobs will necessarily happen in the same order for you as for someone else. Meshing your goals with these checkpoints calls for research and the right tools. That's why I encourage you to work with a planner who understands the possibilities and commits to staying the course with you, reevaluating your plan as necessary. No matter your wealth or stage in life, set out to find a planner you can trust. We all need some help, and the value is beyond simply helping you invest. If someone tells you that you don't have enough wealth to work with them, you're talking to the wrong planner.

The choice of whether to work with a planner or advisor can be a difficult one, especially for investors of my generation. Many people wonder if they could learn to invest on their own. That's a scary idea because it involves spending 40 or 50 hours a week learning about investments and the field of finance in general. But they also have heard stories about people who used an advisor and regretted it later. The point is, choose wisely and work with someone who not only understands your situation now but can also help you create a plan for life and then guide you in checking and adapting it as things arise.

Not all advisors do that, and though life management as a part of financial advising has come a long way since I first started, it remains a serious gap in our industry. I began my financial career in banking and mortgage loans before the 2008 financial crisis but after the dotcom bubble had shaken the public's faith in advisors. In the past decade, however, additional regulations have helped to put boundaries on our industry, along with an increase in registered investment advisors (RIAs), who have a fiduciary responsibility and are governed by the US Securities and Exchange Commission. The right advisor can be an effective guide. Don't be scared to look for one.

Once you have a life plan, you should be calling your planner as you face major changes—*before* you get married or purchase a home. You need to make sure your plan includes your new stage in life. Each decision creates a path forward, which means your plan needs to incorporate it ahead of time, not after the fact. People frequently go through life making huge decisions and notifying their advisor at an annual scheduled meeting. The change is noted; then they move on.

That's not good enough. In the real game of Life, you're not at the mercy of a spinner. You make decisions, and you can readjust your plan to accommodate them in advance. You may not be able to anticipate every event—and that's part of the joy of existence—but you can be proactive about many things. If your life becomes complex, your plan should become complex with it. How to do that will be the subject of the rest of this book.

CHECKLIST

- ✅ *Do you have a plan?*
- ✅ *What's in it?*
- ✅ *Have you set goals for yourself?*

2

HOW DO YOU KNOW
IF YOUR PLAN IS WORKING?

Last year, I gave more than 20 presentations about financial market overviews, planning, and strategies to prospective investors and other advisors. Each time I give a presentation, I ask the crowd, "How many of you have a financial plan?" More than half the room raises their hands. Then I ask a follow-up question: "How many of you benchmark your investments?" Benchmarking investments—checking performance against expected returns—is a common practice in the financial industry. Nearly everyone raises their hands. Then I follow up with another question: "How many of you benchmark your financial plan?" No one raises a hand . . . ever.

Think about that. In the financial industry, we monitor every aspect of performance and fees annually, if not more often. However, when it comes to a financial plan that dictates the what, why, how, when, and where for your life goals, it seems that no one checks on it regularly.

At an event hosted by Barron's for the top 1 percent of independent advisors, the host of the meeting made a bold statement that confirmed what I'd been thinking: "Financial plans are irrelevant the day after they're made." All around the room, I saw attendees questioning this premise. He's right, though. Every day that you spend, save, or do something that changes your goals means that your plan has changed. You need to know how your overall goals are being met, not just what's happening with your investments. For instance, did you intend to pay off your mortgage in 20 years instead of 30? Are you on track to reach this goal? Will your situation allow you to pay it off sooner, or has it forced you to pull back?

To check every aspect of a plan may seem daunting, but it's important because this isn't just a plan on paper. It's your life. You probably already have benchmarks for your investments. Most investors have brokerage accounts at a major firm, even if they work with an advisor. Go online to do research, look up quotes, and review fees to see how your various investments have fared.

You can apply the same concept to your overall financial plan yourself or with an advisor. Review your financial plan. Look over the goals you set for the past year, and write down how you performed. Did you save or spend more than expected? Did your investments perform better or worse than expected? After making these notes, ask your advisor to determine if adjustments should be made for the upcoming year.

It's important each year to ask yourself whether your plan would look the same if you created it again from scratch. In my experience, an individual's circumstances change every three years, at least to some extent. Thus, your plan needs to change, even if it requires an overhaul. If you decide to start from scratch and redraft your former plan, this new plan is your benchmark.

When I sit down with someone to discuss a life plan, we always reread our first plan. It's important to be able to look back in five years to see all we have accomplished. We should be five years closer to our goals. It's easy to be shortsighted. That's why a benchmark is important. Think about your investments for a second. Most clients who have an advisor are encouraged to evaluate them over a period of years. As in the board game of Life, there will be times when we shoot ahead a few extra spaces and other times when we move too slowly. We can adjust our goal to account for that year's underperformance and edit this year's targets to get us back on track. But remember, there's no pass/fail grade. The point is to keep to a life plan that suits you.

Any life plan has to take into consideration your needs, wants, and dreams. Those are the subject of the next chapter.

CHECKLIST

- Have you finalized your plan?
- Have you checked to see how your investments have fared?
- When did you last update your plan?
- How often are you reviewing/updating it?

3

DEFINING YOUR GOALS—YOUR NEEDS, WANTS, AND DREAMS

Dr. Sam Smith (not his real name) and his wife were introduced to me through a client referral. They had an interesting story: Sam, a surgeon, was in his late 60s. He had spent most of his career making more than $500,000 a year. In addition, his wife worked and earned a decent income. As we went through their goals, they told me that they had considered retirement only during the past year. He wanted to work until he didn't enjoy it anymore, and they always assumed they'd have enough funds.

As I looked at their assets, however, I quickly saw they didn't have much saved and still weren't saving much. The good thing was they had no debt. However, like many people, they "lived up" to their income, paying for nice cars, private schools for their kids, expensive college tuitions, and extravagant vacations around the world. They had three properties for family use, including their main residence, and planned to pass these down to their children. When I asked about their needs, they listed all these things.

It took a long session of going through their whole plan to show them they needed to sell two of the properties to have a better chance of outliving their money in retirement. They could offer to sell the properties to their children, but that was the only choice unless Sam wanted to work eight more years, into his mid-70s.

The Smiths' story is a great example of how important it is to prioritize needs, goals, and dreams and to incorporate them into a financial plan. They had an income that would allow them to achieve all those things, but they had decided to enjoy life to the fullest in the present instead of planning for the future. Of course, you *should* enjoy life with your family. However, striking a balance ensures you aren't playing catch-up late in life.

Financial stress is a constant for most of us, and it's one of the largest obstacles blocking our happiness. One way to overcome it is to know where we stand in our life plan. Are we keeping up, exceeding it, or falling behind? By knowing how we are doing, we can make adjustments, improve our position, and get rid of what keeps us up at night.

An important part of any plan is to set our goals in terms of understanding our needs, wants, and dreams. We all have them.

The most important and necessary goals are your needs. The next level of importance are your wants, and the goals you reach for are your dreams. The hardest part of a plan is to have an honest conversation about how to prioritize these goals. Write all your goals down on paper. Once you have a list, begin to rank them in importance. At this point, having another set of eyes is important and can make a big difference. Keep in mind that an overall need—providing for a family, for example—will always be the same, though the amount needed to accomplish that may change as your family grows.

Think back to the imaginary board game of your real life at the beginning of the book. Needs should get the most attention because you won't be able to make any move without them. Think of wants as extras that move you ahead more quickly or more comfortably. And dreams? Maybe that's a reward if you land on certain spaces or if you get to the last space sooner than the other players.

Start with your most basic long-term goal—that is your first need. For most of us, it's to be able to retire, because we'll lose the ability to work at some point. The need is clear for all of us, but our individual financial details will differ.

The Smiths agreed on their priorities. It was clear they could achieve them, if their investments reached 5 percent a year. However, we had to take into account potential bad years in the market. In that case, they could choose not to go on their two extravagant annual vacations. They could eat out less and cut down on a lot of their "fun" items. Pulling back on these things meant they only needed a 2 percent return on their investments. They could get that from dividends and interest, without having to take money from their principal.

I won't tell you what other goals should be considered needs. That's up to you. What I will say is that your children's education should *not* be one of them. This may sound controversial or make you question this book, but, trust me, I have seen successful business owners, surgeons, and even wealthy politicians squander money on this goal, putting it before their retirement or other needs.

The Smiths, for example, earned millions but spent a great deal of it on education. When we added the costs together, private school alone cost them roughly $540,000 for their three children. College tuition cost another $600,000. They spent these funds instead of investing them. To them, it was 100 percent worth it, and they have no regrets. They were fortunate, however, that Sam still had a strong and steady income.

Of course, your children are important, and they add purpose to your life. I get it. I have beautiful daughters myself. But anyone—and I mean anyone—can borrow for college. No one can borrow for retirement. You need to make sure your retirement and other basic needs *always* are met first before any dollar goes into a college savings account. College or private school education goes into the wants category.

Wants may include the ability to travel once a year or play golf once a month. These goals become priorities *after* your needs are met. You cannot put funds toward these goals until you have fully covered your needs. In the example above, we could meet all of the Smiths' needs with investments that generated 2 percent of their income. To cover wants, let's say you need an additional 1.5 percent. That means, from an investment standpoint, you need to generate an income of 3.5 percent to cover both needs and wants. That percentage is still in a fairly conservative range for a rate of return. We can achieve this with low-risk, fixed-income investments.

Suppose we want to aim higher to accomplish our dreams, however—at a goal of 6 percent. Doing that while protecting your principal may be tougher to achieve, but it's possible by investing the additional amount in a more risky fund, such as dividend-paying equities.

All of your final aspirations should be considered dreams. These are your stretch goals—beyond your needs and even your wants. Instead of traveling once a year, maybe you want to travel three times and go first class. Instead of golfing on a monthly basis, maybe you envision getting a country club membership with your buddies.

Dividing your goals into needs, wants, and dreams is a useful tool and should be part of your life planning. Work with your partner or spouse, if you have one, because you may find that some of your needs, wants, and dreams are not the same. What you may consider wants may be considered needs by your spouse, and vice versa. However, the agreed-upon needs are your highest priority. That's where your first dollars should go because they serve as the foundation on which your life plan will be built and regularly evaluated. If you're working with a life planner or advisor, he or she will be able to help you adapt the plan as your goals—your needs, wants, and dreams—change. That's why your plan should have built-in checkpoints that reflect major events, planned or not.

We'll touch on those checkpoints in Part Three of this book. First, though, we need to address some of the financial tools you'll need to review when you hit the important milestones of your life.

CHECKLIST

- ⊘ *Have you prioritized your goals?*
- ⊘ *What are your needs?*
- ⊘ *What are your wants?*
- ⊘ *What are your dreams?*

PART 2

FINANCIAL PLANNING— SOME BASICS

4

YOU NEED A BUDGET

My wife and I had very different views on budgeting when we first married. I was brought up with the concept of save first, spend later. That was ingrained in me by my parents, who always saved and insisted that any spending had to be justified. My wife grew up differently. For her it was spend first, then maybe save.

We struggled with budgeting early on. Before we were married, I built up savings and bought a house, and we both bought cars when we were engaged. While I worked long hours and began studying for additional accreditations in my industry, I trusted her to pay all the bills and keep our finances in line. It wasn't until six months later, after I had passed a difficult exam, that I logged into our bank account to check on its status. I was shocked to find out that our savings had shrunk. I was upset, but the situation didn't faze my wife.

We had to have a heart-to-heart conversation. She didn't understand the purpose of not living paycheck to paycheck until I sat down and created a financial plan in front of her. When we looked at all of our expenses over the past few months, it seemed 50 percent of them were discretionary and easily manageable. Still, the process wasn't easy. My wife used to call budgeting the "b" word. She hated when I brought up the topic, but we had to find a way to make it work. Eventually, we created a system we could both live with and that gave each of us peace of mind. Now we're on the same page and save more than we spend.

Our company hires anywhere from 6 to 12 interns a semester. We have yet to meet one who has been taught budgeting or financial planning. That's a large gap in knowledge, and few schools address it. A mentor of mine likes to say, "Experience is the comb life gives us after we have lost our hair." That's often true about learning to manage money; for many people, the lessons come too late.

Part of budgeting is understanding cash flow, which is a foreign topic for most individuals. The first question to ask yourself is: Does my personal income statement show more inflows than outflows? In other words, is there more money coming in than going out? Too many people don't know their monthly cash flow. If you're not confident that your cash flow is positive, that's a matter of concern. You may not be stressed now, but the pressure will build if you continue to drop into negative cash flow territory.

Cash flow is a combination of budgeting and debt management, which we'll get to in the following chapter. The first step, however, is to make a list of your recurring debts. The items should be your necessities—a place to live, utilities, a reasonable amount for food, transportation, and other must-haves. There will be some room to increase or decrease these items. It's okay if you're inaccurate the first month you begin monitoring your expenses. Are you comfortably paying these expenses each month? How much of your income is left after you account for these necessities?

The second step is to make a list of where any extra income is going and to prioritize those items. Are you making the mistake of putting fun things like recreation and travel before savings? The Smiths tried this tactic and had to play catch-up later. They had ample income and time to grow their nest egg for retirement but put it off until they were nearing the end of their working lives.

Many individuals make the mistake of going through a cash-flow analysis and using what's left over to put into retirement or savings. Instead, you should build the plan based on how much you need for the retirement you want. These dollars are your needs—or at least your most important wants.

The third step is to work your way to a positive cash flow statement each month. The goal is to have more money coming in than going out, even after putting away money you need for retirement. Try it for one month. Once you accomplish it for a month, make it two, then three. Eventually you'll be motivated to keep a positive cash flow your whole life.

To help you budget, check out some great resources, including a very useful app called YNAB, which you can find at www.youneedabudget.com. Along with ways to keep track of your money, the site emphasizes that budgeting—like a life plan—is an evolving process and not a pass/fail one-time course.

EMERGENCY SAVINGS

In 2017, 34 percent of US households experienced a major, unexpected expense, according to a Bankrate financial security index survey. Only 39 percent of Americans said they would be able to cover even a $1,000 emergency. Don't get caught in that bind!

Every financial plan should start with emergency savings. It's the foundation of your financial future and well-being. Imagine trying to build a home without a foundation; it wouldn't last long. Similarly, you're not on steady footing if you don't have some savings in the bank for a rainy day. And inevitably, there's a rainy day.

A lot of experts claim that the equivalent of three to six months of your salary is enough for an emergency savings account. I don't agree. First, the most common reason people dip into their savings is because they lost a job. In that case, it's doubtful that three to six months will be enough time for you to get back on your feet. Job losses are typically unexpected and may affect a large group of people.

No one predicted the financial crisis in 2008 or the energy crisis in 2015 that led to nearly 9 million lost jobs. All those people needed jobs at the same time, and the market offered slim pickings. The unemployed were left with three choices: accept a job with lower wages, compete with hundreds of applicants for the same type of job, or, with enough savings, take the time to find suitable work.

Another problem with the three-to-six-month rule is that it doesn't necessarily account for your actual expenses. Your emergency savings account should focus on your personal needs rather than merely your salary. For example, a single 23-year-old won't have the same expenses as a married 50-year-old with two children in college and a few dogs. Even if they make the same amount of money, the latter will have more monthly expenses. That means he or she will need more money in his emergency savings account.

Here are a few tips to help you decide the exact amount you should have in emergency funds:

- If you're already saving for retirement, subtract that from your total net income.

- Examine the rest of your income and consider the following: What are your *needs* and what are your *wants*? The two do not always coincide. Focus only on your needs.

- Know your industry. How common are layoffs, and how does your industry weather a recession? Is three to six months a realistic estimate of how long you'll be out of work? This will determine how long emergency funds should cover your needs.

- Once you've figured out how much you and your family *need* to live on and for how long, create a plan on how to save and get there.

- Ultimately, when it comes to emergency savings, thinking about worst-case scenarios is the best approach. What would happen if you lost your job, a family member got sick, or you were involved in a tragic accident? You may settle on a number that exceeds three to six months of salary, but better to be safe than sorry.

If it's hard for you to do the math, you could also simplify the calculation by using the pillow test—my go-to test for anything related to finances. At night, when stress keeps you from falling asleep, listen to that feeling. If you cannot sleep because you believe you don't have enough savings, it's time to add to that bank account.

The good news is that if you're still working, you've time left to save for any emergency that might come your way. The funds to cover the unexpected are achievable. Start building your savings now.

Don't be satisfied with just three months' salary. Focus on your needs over a longer horizon—you'll be happy you did.

Making a budget is crucial at every stage of your life. Many people struggle to balance their income with their outflows. But you can start by focusing on one month at a time. Can you control your spending? Then, can you bring in more income than you spend? Once you have done it for a month, challenge yourself to a second and a third month. Continue until you have a lifestyle with a positive money flow. That will be the first step to creating a strong life plan.

CHECKLIST

- ✅ *Do you have a budget?*
- ✅ *If not, what are your expenses, and what is your monthly income after taxes?*
- ✅ *Are you spending more than you're earning?*

5

MANAGING YOUR DEBT

Most of us have experienced debt. We purchase cars or houses, take out student loans, and use credit cards for groceries and other goods. There's not necessarily anything wrong with borrowing. After all, how many of us could pay cash for a house early in our careers?

The way we should manage debt depends on where we're at in our lives. The important thing is to always keep an eye on our balance sheet and make changes if they become necessary. For example, I met with a couple whom I'll call Corey and Sandy Wallens. They were in their early 40s with debts including a home mortgage, two cars, a student loan, and credit cards. They had two children and wanted to discuss college planning and ways to save more for retirement. As I looked at their budget, however, some problems were immediately apparent. The student loan and credit card interest rates were extremely high. It was going to be tough to repay them. At least the home interest rate was still near an all-time low, and that became part of the solution.

DEBT	INTEREST RATE
Home	3.75%
Car 1	3.95%
Car 2	4.15%
Student Loan	7.00%
Credit Card	18.60%

When we examined how to improve the Wallenses' balance sheet, there was room to move the credit card and student debt into the home debt. We were able to refinance the credit card and student debt into a home loan at 4.25 percent. In addition, they could write off a portion on their taxes. For couples in their 30s and 40s, this is a normal balance sheet.

In this case, relieving some of the debt wasn't difficult. It just required some time to examine what was happening with their finances. But time is short for all of us. Individuals tend to delay focusing on these types of debts until they are in their peak earning years toward the middle or late stages of their career. That is typically when folks begin to plan for retirement and want to pay off debts. In reality, however, managing debt should be a lifelong task. You can start right away.

Early in our lives, it's useful and necessary to acquire homes, cars, and other large assets. Closer to retirement, we may want to pay off debts. In retirement, debt can become a burdensome outflow.

The most important point is to adopt the mindset of tackling your debt before you sign loan papers. Individuals struggle when they jump into debt without a plan. Taking on too much debt forces them to become a hamster in a wheel, forever struggling to keep up.

Remember, all debt is not bad debt, and planning allows you to use debt in your favor. That may mean not paying off debts and using the money for a worthwhile investment, like building up the other side of your balance sheet. Paying off your debts may mean you miss out on potential opportunities.

Let's look at the Wallenses as an example. They inherited $100,000 and considered using it to pay down a chunk of their mortgage. I asked them if they had considered investing the $100,000 instead. It never crossed their mind. I recommended we go over the numbers to determine the best approach. If they invested the $100,000 and received a 5 percent return over 15 years, the investment would be worth nearly $208,000. If the return were 8 percent, the value would be slightly more than $317,000 instead.

The other option was to pay down the loan. Their current payment was $1,389. If they paid it down and were able to refinance it at the exact same rate of 3.75 percent, the payment dropped to $926. That's a difference of $473 a month. Let's say they invested the difference in the payment into the market at the same rates of return. The future value at 5 percent would be about $128,000, and the value at 8 percent would be roughly $166,000.

Because they were able to refinance their mortgage at a low interest rate, it enabled them to invest the funds. Now their retirement fund and the equity in their house are growing simultaneously.

What is good debt? I grew up in Texas and always thought of our home merely as a place to live. That was a common perspective among most families where I lived. No one viewed a home as an asset. My parents and others of their generation focused on paying off their mortgage as fast as possible. There was a downside, however, since this limited other assets and removed opportunities to invest in other ways—for example, in rental properties.

What's most important to remember is that everyone's situation is unique. Paying off debts quickly may be right for some people, but there may be advantages to keeping to a schedule and building other assets. Everyone needs to find the right balance for their own situation. That is why having a plan is crucial and why you should revisit it before making any decision about taking on debt.

AVOIDING HIGHER INTEREST PAYMENTS

When interest rates make headlines, we tend to focus on the impact on our investments. That's easy to do when you hear some pundits claim rising rates help them, while others say exactly the opposite. But don't forget about the other side of your balance sheet. If you carry any type of debt, interest rates can have a notable effect on your financial well-being.

Think about the Wallenses and their debt. Fortunately, they were able to lower their interest rate. Even better, however, is to avoid getting into a sticky situation.

Now is the time to make sure that all your debt is at a fixed, not adjustable, interest rate. If your credit cards have a balance, focus on paying them off now to avoid monthly interest, which is probably an adjustable interest rate. The more you can protect yourself against increasing interest payments, the better off you will be.

In fact, if you have any type of debt, it is time to look closely and see if any of the rates are subject to increase. Don't be put off by those disclaimers that seem to be 1,000 pages long and printed in illegible two-point type. To avoid being intimidated by the fine print, follow these steps to understand your debt:

- Learn the base rates of your debts.
- Understand how the rates on the debt instrument are affected by increases and decreases.
- Is your rate fixed or adjustable? If rates increase, does your interest payment also increase?
- Find out if there is a prepayment penalty.
- Is there an interest-free borrowing period you can take advantage of?
- Can you borrow for a month, pay it back, and not be charged any interest?
- Can you refinance the debt? For example, can you refinance your credit card debt into a mortgage (for example, refinancing a credit card rate of 18 percent into a 5 percent mortgage)?

Take an adjustable-rate mortgage with a spread plus 1 Year LIBOR (London Interbank Offering Rate). If you are in the adjustable period or about to adjust, your payment is likely to go up. An increase of 1 percent on a mortgage interest rate of 4 percent on a mortgage loan of $200,000 can increase your monthly payment by $100 to $140.

With credit cards or loans, if there is no prepayment penalty, it may work to your advantage to pay them off early or consolidate the debt into one loan. If you must use a credit card for a purchase you cannot pay off the same month, look for a credit card with a 0 percent interest period. It will be easier to pay down a large balance over 12 months if no interest is charged.

The rates on payday loans also increase. If you depend on these loans, you may find yourself in a vicious cycle, since these rates are commonly renewed every two weeks or once a month.

For any debt instrument, when interest rates rise, so will the rates that affect you. If you are considering purchasing a home, a car, or any other large asset, get a fixed-rate loan. If you aren't sure about the exact timing, budget your payments with the assumption of a higher interest rate. This way you will be prepared for the future. If you have debts with different interest rates, begin paying down the highest one first, *especially* if it is adjustable!

Managing your debt is a useful part of your budgeting process. The key is knowing what you signed up for and checking on it regularly so that you are in control.

CHECKLIST

- ✓ *Can you list your debts (credit cards, student loan, car loan, mortgage, etc.)?*
- ✓ *Do you know the interest rate you're paying and how it works?*
- ✓ *Which debts should you pay down first?*

6

INVESTING

Here's a cautionary tale: A few years ago, I worked with a client—let's call him Al—who was aggressive when it came to investments. He wanted the highest returns with what he believed to be the lowest amount of risk. Al took most of his money to follow an unproven market-timing fund that was supposed to protect investors in a bad economy and do well in a good economy. The risk is these kinds of strategies may work in theory when you examine past market conditions, but they rarely work that way in the future. Each down market is unique.

Al was on pace to retire the following year. I had emphasized to him the importance of transitioning his money to safer, income-producing investments that would remove the stock market risk. Al ignored me. He insisted on doing what he thought would make him wealthier faster.

This was a common story during the financial crisis. Six months after Al reconfigured his portfolio, his investments were down 20 percent. And even after the market rebounded, his portfolio did not. He had to postpone his goal of retirement for four years. Al was fortunate that a good market followed and he was able to retire at all.

If he had carried the same type of risk in a recession, his situation would have been more dire.

Investing can be a scary subject. As with all aspects of your life plan, the key is to set goals and reevaluate where you are at the checkpoints of your life. It helps if you work with an advisor who can help you focus on aspects of investing that most apply to you.

20-year annualized returns by asset class (1999–2018)

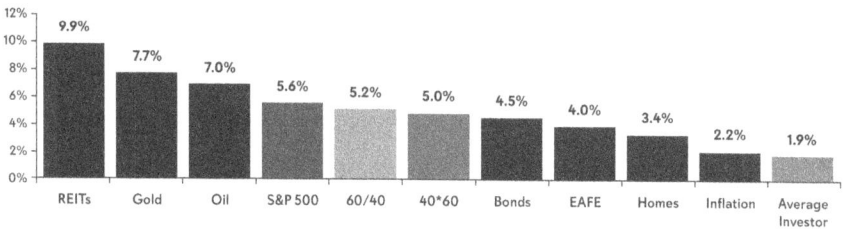

Source: JPMorgan Asset Managment; (Top) Barclays, Bloomberg, FactSet, Standard & Poor's; (Bottom) Dalbar Inc.
Indices used are as follows: REITS: NAREIT Equity REIT Index, EAFE: MSCI EAFE, Oil: WTI Index, Bonds: Bloomberg Barclays US Aggregate Index, Homes: median sale price of existing single-family homes, Gold: USD/troy oz., Inflation: CPI. 60/40: A balanced portfolio with 60% invested in S&P 500 Index and 40% invested in high-quality US fixed income, represented by the Bloomberg Barclays US Aggregate Index. The portfolio is rebalanced annually. Average asset allocation investor return is based on an analysis by Dalbar Inc., which utilizes the net of aggregate mutual fund sales, redemptions, and exchanges each month as a measure of investor behavior. Returns are annualized (and total return where applicable) and represent the 20-year period ending 12/31/18 to match Dalbar's most recent analysis. *Guide to the Markets* – US Data are as of March 31, 2019.

Republished with permission from JPMorgan Chase & Co. (c) 2020

It may be tempting to think that you can read books and articles and handle your own investments. But as you can see from the previous chart, the average person's investments do not perform nearly as well as the market or a diversified portfolio. In general, the self-directed investors who do well work at it full time, spending more than 40 hours a week on their portfolio. It becomes their profession and their passion. However, for most of us it is hard to take emotion out of investing and to follow a rules-based system. It can be difficult to watch the daily volatility of the market. That is why many individuals seek an advisor in the first place. They are seeking peace of mind and hoping someone else can manage their portfolio rationally and appropriately to achieve their long-term goals.

In reality, there is no secret, all-encompassing approach to investing. Your outcome will be better the earlier you invest, due to the gifts of time and compounding.

Not long ago, I worked for discount brokerage firms. Most of the clients at these firms chose their own investments. They were confident in their strategies, but rarely did those work out as imagined. In fact, fewer than 5 percent of the self-directed investors performed better than a diversified portfolio. The more complex the strategy they tried to implement, the more risk they incurred. The best investors were the ones who were less active, diligently researched investments before purchasing them, and held them for the intermediate and long term.

There's a common motto in the financial world—Keep It Simple Stupid (KISS)—and it applies to investments. Simple investments are boring; they do not produce exciting results. You are not going to turn $1,000 into $100 million by choosing boring investments like index funds or a diversified portfolio. However, you also will not lose all of your money. Simple investments provide a return without the unnecessary risks that disturb your peace of mind.

An index fund can be a mutual fund or exchange-traded fund (ETF) like SPDR S&P 500 (SPY). The benefit of a mutual fund that invests in an index is you can increase your shares by making monthly purchases. As you get closer to retirement, you should transition the portfolio to a more conservative type. Why? We have seen major down markets in 2000 to 2002 and 2008. A decrease of 40 percent in your retirement funds the year before you retire will hurt your plan. Ideally, five years before retirement, your plan should only need a small return in your investments to reach your goal—not a high-risk, high-return investment.

Let's go back to needs, wants, and dreams. For instance, you need to earn 4 percent on investments to achieve all three goals. The needs portion should be invested in conservative instruments. In the current environment, we can invest in short-term CDs for 2 to 2.4 percent. We can take a little more risk and invest in corporate bonds to earn closer to 4 percent. After accounting for needs, we can review your wants and dreams and take on a little more risk to earn a higher yield. For wants, we could look at dividend-paying equities such as utilities. The price can fluctuate, but the yield can range from 4 to 6 percent in this category.

To meet dream goals, we can add some exposure to real estate investment trusts, master limited partnerships, high-yield fixed income, or other higher-income-paying instruments. Even if the economy were to experience a significant downturn, your needs would still be addressed. The investments tabbed for wants and dreams may fluctuate, but you'll have the flexibility to ride it out. This approach allows you to turn the television off, forget about the market, and sleep well at night.

CHECKLIST

- ✅ *Are you investing for retirement?*
- ✅ *How are you investing for retirement?*
- ✅ *Are you diversified according to your risk level?*

7

LIFE INSURANCE

Have you ever had an interview where you've been asked about the biggest struggle you've faced? I have. Although I know that the question is supposed to address my life at work, it usually makes me think of the real difficulties that have confronted my family.

I remember three tough events, in particular, as if they happened yesterday. The first was on New Year's Day 1995. My brother passed away in a car crash. The second was in 1996, when our house burned down while my mom was taking us to school. The third took place five years later, when my younger brother was diagnosed with a rare form of cancer. Events like these can break a family or bring it closer together. They all had long-lasting impacts on our family.

In each case, however, we were helped through the crisis financially by the fact that my parents had insurance. Rebuilding a home can be astronomically expensive. Three years of daily medical care can cost even more. And the pain of mourning a family member should not be exacerbated by the burden of medical bills and funeral fees.

Most Americans would probably agree that the average person needs insurance, but we usually don't think in terms of worst-case scenarios. When we purchase a home, we focus on the excitement of a new living space. When we buy a car, we relish the pleasure of driving it around. Insurance is like plumbing in a house. It's out of sight and out of mind . . . until a pipe breaks.

The hard part is knowing how much insurance—and what kind—is enough. If you have a family and you're the sole breadwinner, then life insurance isn't optional. You need it to guarantee your family will be taken care of in the event of your death. A discussion about insurance is called for the moment a spouse or children enter the picture. (Those are important checkpoints we'll discuss later.)

Insurance is a contract in which the purchaser pays a premium to receive protection against certain events. Life insurance, for example, protects your family and beneficiaries in the case of your death by providing them with a lump-sum payment to make up for potential lost income. The policy can be kept until age 100, as long as the premium payments are made. The hard part is sustaining those payments without a regular income, as in retirement.

Permanent life insurance (which covers whole, universal, and variable life insurance) can also be bought as an investment. It comes with high management expenses and commissions but contains a tax-deferred growth benefit. You can pay any funds into this insurance plan that you want to pass down to your beneficiaries; the death benefit will be tax free. You can also borrow against a policy's cash value in case of emergency or to make a down payment on a house. This is similar to obtaining a loan or line of credit.

In rare cases, one can actually receive a portion of the death benefit for health purposes if your policy allows for accelerated benefits. However, in that case, you give up a portion or all of the death benefit.

Term life insurance works differently because it has a specific duration. For example, 20-year term life insurance means the policy expires in 20 years. The client will pay a premium throughout the life of the policy to have coverage. When the policy expires, all money paid will be forfeited. The advantage is that because there's no cash value and it's not an investment, payments for term insurance are usually much lower.

As you investigate life insurance, start by checking out any employee benefits you might have. Some firms offer insurance with the payment deducted from your paycheck. Employers may even provide supplemental benefits up to a specific dollar amount or to a multiple of your salary. It is an additional cost but may be cheaper than seeking an outside policy. Of course, you can also seek an independent policy directly through an insurance provider.

For the breadwinner of a family with young children, the payment for a life insurance policy with a death benefit of $200,000 may be affordable but probably does not provide enough protection. In that case, term insurance may be the answer. The premiums will be cheaper than for universal life policies, but the payout may be 10 times greater. The difference between $200,000 and $2,000,000 in the case of tragedy is huge. Yes, you are giving up the cash value in the policy, but the cash value at the end of 10 years or even 20 years is not that big.

A year ago, I met a woman whose husband had recently died in a car wreck on the way to work. He supported the family with a good income while she stayed home, but they had incurred a lot of debt from two properties and new cars. With two kids in college and another in high school, she was petrified because they only had $100,000 in life insurance. She didn't know what to do or even where to start. Her husband had done a decent job of saving, but there was not enough to cover debt payments and living expenses for his wife and children after he was gone. The cost for this couple to obtain a term life insurance policy would have been just $35 monthly. This was less than what they spent on one of their weekly family dinners at a restaurant.

Why do many insurance agents and advisors recommend permanent life insurance policies? The answer is that they get higher commissions.

Still, there are times when a universal, variable, or whole life insurance policy makes sense. One example is a policy on your children, for whom term insurance doesn't apply. It hurts to think that something tragic may happen, but bad things happen and they can be costly. Some life insurance policies allow you to convert them to cover medical expenses, and that can be worth it.

If you have an ultra-high net worth and want to minimize your heirs' estate taxes, a permanent life insurance policy also may provide a benefit. It is important to work with your life planner to understand what policy is best for you.

Remember, however, insurance policies are not good investment vehicles. Insurance is meant to be a risk-mitigating tool for major life events such as death, injury, sickness, and so on. Annuities and insurance products usually pay commissions up front, which is the reason advisors who are licensed insurance agents may recommend these products. Once they've sold you the product, they move on to the next client because little compensation exists for long-term relationships. They are not affected if you cancel the product, which often carries a hefty penalty.

Consider instead an exchange-traded fund (ETF). Unlike an annuity, you aren't locked into an ETF, and there is no penalty for getting out of it earlier. If you invest in an annuity, you are committed to the investment for a period of 7 to 15 years. To get out of the investment before the lock-up period ends, you have to pay a penalty, and that can be significant.

It is important to read any contract before signing it. Take your time, research it, and understand it before committing to insurance or an annuity as an investment.

CALCULATE YOUR LIFE INSURANCE NEEDS

How much life insurance do you need? The answer depends on your family, current age, target retirement age, and income.

Here's a quick example of how to calculate the correct amount: If you're 35 and plan to retire at 65, then you have 30 years of future income to protect. If you earn $50,000/year, you would likely want to have at least 30 times that number in life insurance ($1,500,000). That calculation obviously doesn't account for the taxes you pay on income and retirement contributions, so be sure to subtract those amounts when you work the equation. Now grab a pencil and try it out for yourself:

1. Pick a target retirement date.

2. Figure out your income after retirement contributions and income taxes.

3. Multiply the years left before retirement by the income you calculated in step 2.

4. Review your assets. Deduct these from the total calculated in step 3. (*Do not include your home as an asset.*)

5. The total number after step 4 is the amount of life insurance you need to have.

Is there a difference between the number you just calculated and the number on your current policy? If so, don't be too concerned—you can take steps to close the gap, especially if you're still young. With term insurance, for example, the earlier you start, the cheaper it can be. For example, a healthy 30-year-old can obtain a $1 million 20-year policy for roughly $40 a month.

It's a tough thing to watch a family lose a spouse or parent. It's even tougher if there is only minimal life insurance for immediate or future expenses. That $40 could mean the difference between having to return to work after losing a loved one, or not.

Understanding your insurance needs (and how to meet them) does not need to be daunting. It's just one of the basic financial tools that underpin your plan in your personal game of Life.

CHECKLIST

- ✓ *Do you have life insurance? What kind is it?*
- ✓ *Have you had any life changes that might impact your life insurance?*
- ✓ *Is it enough to support your family, if you have one?*

8

TAX PLANNING

Whether your income is high or minimum wage, we all have to pay taxes. No matter who you are or what you do, Uncle Sam will be a part of your life.

The younger we are, the less we tend to focus on taxes. Most of us have jobs, and our income is reflected on our W-2 forms when tax time rolls around. The accountant in the family collects the W-2s, or perhaps we calculate taxes with an online software program. There isn't much to it. As we get older and have a family, build a career, and accumulate wealth, tax planning becomes more important and more complex. There may be multiple sources of income and reasons to pay attention to tax regulations in order to allow for growth of assets.

You may be reading this book and saying to yourself, *I don't have a high income or a lot of assets, so this chapter isn't for me.* With all due respect, that's not the best way to think about it. Though the regulations may change every year, credits and deductions exist for people of all income levels. Too many individuals and families miss out on benefits meant for them.

The most common question I get during tax-planning discussions is "What's better, a tax credit or deduction?" The answer is simple: a tax credit. A deduction offsets your gross income, while a tax credit is applied directly against your taxes. Moreover, a tax credit for a lower-income family can have a significant impact. For example, a $3,000 tax credit for a family earning $60,000 is more significant than a $3,000 tax credit for a family earning $160,000.

The real issue, though, is that you should do your research and take advantage of the credits or deductions to which you are entitled. Taxes are part of the review process at every checkpoint in your life, as we'll see in Part Three.

Tax laws are complicated, and they change every year. If it's not your profession, it's hard to keep up with the changes that can impact you annually. The tax laws that took effect in 2017 made it better to take the standard deduction, unless you can itemize your deductions to a dollar amount more than the standard deduction. Itemizing all expenses and deductions throughout the year may allow you to get a higher deduction on your taxes at year end. The goal is to take the higher of the two to offset as much of your income as possible so your tax bill is lower. These amounts will continue to move up and down throughout your life, and that's another reason why it's important to stay up to date with these changes.

Retirement is a huge checkpoint and a place where tax planning is crucial, since that's when we begin living off our investments instead of our employment income. Our current laws allow us to count dividends and income from passive investments as capital gains taxed at 15 or 20 percent. If most of your assets are in qualified retirement accounts such as a 401k or IRA, the distributions will be treated as ordinary income and taxed at your current tax rate, which will be at a lower rate for most people. That's all the more reason to carefully consider where you place your money.

Some investors hate paying taxes so much that they may make unprofitable decisions. Earlier this year, I met with a client named Elly about her portfolio. She held tax-free investments that paid income. One of them was an individual bond for which she paid $100,000. The price for this investment had risen 8 percent. I pointed out to her that she could sell it and reinvest the $108,000 in a new investment paying the exact same tax-free income.

"No, don't sell it," she said. She didn't want to pay taxes on the gain.

"Your income will still be the same, and you'll have a profit," I told her. "If you hold the bond until maturity, the price will return to par, and you'll end up with no gain and the same amount of interest."

Elly couldn't get past the fact that she might have to pay $2,800 in taxes (based on her effective tax rate of 35 percent on the $8,000 gain), despite the fact that she would have earned $5,200 after taxes.

I see this all the time. Clients may have an investment that has risen in value but is beginning to decline. Ideally, they should sell the asset to lock in the gain, but the idea of paying taxes is too distasteful. The investor ends up riding the investment all the way back down rather than walking away a winner.

TAX-FREE INVESTING

Many investors try to reduce their April 15 bill by seeking tax-free investments such as municipal bonds. Firms that specialize in tax-free investing will use that as a selling point. But for families in many lower and middle tax brackets, the corporate bond market may actually outperform tax-free municipals on an after-tax basis.

As an investor, you need to compare both products against your effective tax rate. If you don't know that rate, take a look at the past year's tax return.

For example, a tax-free municipal bond may pay 2.5 percent, while a corporate bond pays 4.25 percent for a similar credit rating and maturity. Let's consider a client who has an effective tax rate of 30 percent. If we take the after-tax basis of the corporate bond, the yield is 2.975 percent. This is more than the municipal bond, making it the preferable investment.

It's important to look at the return or income net of taxes. We call it the tax-equivalent yield. I had a client, Harry, who loved the idea of tax-free investments. He invested in municipal bonds, which produced tax-free income. His father recommended these investments to him when he was younger, and Harry stuck with them.

However, yields and tax rates changed over the years. Harry's tax rate was 25 percent. The current yield for new municipal bonds was an average of 2 percent. The corporate bond yield was 4 percent; after taxes, it was 3 percent. For Harry, this was a full percent higher in income after taxes. So, he recognized the benefit of changing his strategy. Since his portfolio was $1 million, he was able to give himself a $10,000 raise. That meant he was able to take his wife on a trip of her choice.

Calculations like these should be taken into account as part of your ongoing financial planning instead of just for portfolio management. For example, you may want to sell investments to realize tax losses to carry forward and offset other appreciating assets. A business owner who wants to sell his or her company may be looking for some loss to balance a gain. Or a homeowner may contemplate selling a home or property that increased in value. Other considerations include: What happens to the money realized by any sale? Will you put it in a similar investment? Are there transaction fees? Taxes on gains in the future?

Another important consideration is asset location. Investing in certain assets in an IRA versus a normal brokerage account can help avoid tax drag. Tax drag is the amount earned on an investment compared to the same gain after being taxed. In a taxable account with annual rebalancing or trading, the tax drag increases with a higher time horizon or higher return. It's lower for a tax-deferred account when distribution is taxed only once. This is not a consideration for a tax-exempt account, whose funds are invested in an account with after-tax money.

Think of a Roth IRA as a tax-exempt account. You can invest dollars for growth investments into this portfolio for the long term. Some investments have different tax treatments. Individual bonds pay interest at ordinary income rates; dividends are paid at long-term capital gains rates. Under today's tax rules, dividends are taxed at a lower rate than interest. That means you'd want to earn interest in an IRA account and dividends in a taxable account, if possible.

Let's say someone recommended a portfolio with 50 percent equities and 50 percent bonds. You had $250,000 in a taxable account and $250,000 in an IRA. It would make sense to put the equities into the taxable account and the bonds into the IRA account.

END-OF-THE-YEAR TAX STRATEGIES

While tax strategies are undoubtedly part of your ongoing financial planning, here's a checklist to go over at the end of the year.

Losses to Offset Income

Our market investments don't always appreciate. It's hard to admit that an investment may have been a mistake, but if the asset is in a taxable account, you can still benefit from it. Review your portfolio and see if you have investments with a current price less than what you paid for it. You can sell these investments and use the losses to potentially offset your investments that appreciated in value. You can sell both positions so the losses offset the gains and avoid a tax liability. This is known as tax-loss harvesting. However, keep in mind that there is one catch: You cannot repurchase the same or "substantially identical" security for 30 days or you will be subject to the Wash Sale rule, which cancels your tax-loss benefit.

Another benefit of taking investment losses is the ability to carry forward any losses you are unable to offset in that year. For example, if you have a loss of $30,000 and a gain of only $20,000, you can offset the gain and carry forward the unused $10,000. Each year, you are allowed to offset ordinary income by $3,000 of this $10,000 until it is all used up.

Gifts and Charitable Contributions

Gifting your investments is a great strategy when your assets have appreciated. You can sell a stock and give cash to charity, but you'll have to pay taxes on what you sell and will have less to give. For example, if you purchased a stock for $50,000 and it's trading at $100,000 by the end of the year, you'll pay taxes on the $50,000 in capital gains if you sell it. For someone in the 25 percent tax bracket, the remaining amount will be $37,500, with $12,500 going to the

IRS. But if you gift the investment to the charity, you can pass along the full amount, including the IRS share.

Tax planning and estate planning tend to overlap. Estates of $11,400,000 or more are subject to estate tax rates that include an inflation adjustment. However, most people forget that it falls to half that on January 1, 2026, unless the provision is extended. With two presidential elections between now and then, politics may play a role in what happens. Unfortunately, many people have ignored other estate-planning laws from which they can benefit because they are focused on the high limit today instead of considering that it might be drastically lower in the future. We'll take a look at estate planning in the next chapter.

What's most important to remember is that tax planning is a vast subject, and it's complicated by the fact that tax laws may change from year to year. That's why it should be an important part of any checkpoint review, both annually and at milestones in your life. Understand how a change in tax law can impact your retirement and estate plans, or any other part of your finances. Shifts in the law can put roadblocks on your path, or they can become ways to quickly move you ahead.

CHECKLIST

- ✓ *Have you done any tax planning?*
- ✓ *Do you itemize or take a standard deduction?*
- ✓ *Have you had a life change that impacts your taxes?*
- ✓ *Do you tax-loss harvest?*

9

ESTATE PLANNING

The landscape of estate planning has evolved tremendously over the past few decades. Thirty years ago, the public conversation focused on how to save children and other beneficiaries from paying taxes. Individuals began setting up trusts because the estate tax rate was set at a limit of $600,000, and certain types of trusts allowed investors to remove the assets from their estate for tax purposes. By the 1990s, trusts had become popular as a way of protecting assets against creditors and others.

Everyone eventually leaves this world. The legacy we leave is important. Creating the right estate plan for *you* will depend uniquely on your situation and the goals for your estate. Among other considerations—

- It can vary based on your faith in your children.
- It may depend on whether you have gone through a divorce.
- You may wish to leave something to your grandchildren.
- There may be a charity or organization to which you want to donate.

- You may be worried about protecting your assets from liabilities.

That reminds me of how my parents used to joke that there are four types of people to watch out for: predators, creditors, outlaws, and in-laws. Outlaws or criminals who may steal from us are an obvious threat. However, there are also individuals and businesses who prey on individuals. Creditors may go after an estate before it is distributed to heirs.

Given that half of us will go through a divorce, relations with in-laws may also be worrisome. For any divorced parent, providing for children—whether stepchildren, from a previous marriage, or from a new relationship—becomes exceedingly complex.

Many individuals don't believe they need estate planning, but not preparing for the future can put one's estate at risk. Everyone needs at least a basic will. You can actually go online to create a will or consult with someone to quickly draft one. However, you need to be sure your will can hold up in court.

The hardest part of the estate-planning process is finding someone qualified and trustworthy to work with you. Though many advisors or firms claim to offer this service, they often take a pro forma or standard approach, despite the fact that estate-planning laws are unique to each state. Wealth management and estate planning have also become an opportunity for larger firms to charge higher-than-normal fees to affluent clients who need these services.

A firm may charge a fee for reviewing your estate plan and providing recommendations, but you will still need to see an estate attorney to have the documents drafted. If the advisor is simply providing guidance and not drafting documents, the fee should be part of the financial-planning process. An ad hoc fee for estate planning may be a sign that the advisor is focused more on his or her interest than yours.

Sam and Janet are clients of ours with three adult children. Two of the adult children are still somewhat dependent on the parents and have not mastered the art of budgeting. Sam and Janet were nervous about their children spending all of their inheritance at once. A will does not provide you with control of the distributions after you have passed, but a trust can do that. We set up a trust for Sam and Janet's estate that provided for assets to pay the children once a year over 10 years instead of all at once.

Each state has unique trust and estate-planning laws. Some have the added benefit of no state income tax. Others may offer more asset protection statutes or have better laws for passing down a legacy.

A dynasty feature allows a trust to provide for several family generations. It can also be used to cover long-term distributions to a charity. Dynasty laws differ from state to state: In Texas, such trusts survive only for 21 years after the death of the last beneficiary. Nevada, on the other hand, allows the trust to continue for 365 years after a beneficiary's passing. A few states set the limit at 1,000 years or let it continue in perpetuity. Any resident of any state can have a trust registered in a different state, as long as the corporate or successor trustee is registered there. You can look for a corporate trustee registered in a state like Nevada, Delaware, South Dakota, or Alaska, which have favorable laws.

Decanting is a feature where new trusts can be set up as subtrusts for someone like a grandchild who may have special needs. Depending on state law, the heir may be able to decant a portion of their inheritance into a special needs trust for the grandchild. Not all states allow this, however.

Trusts and wills are not the only options individuals can use for estate planning. Family limited partnerships (FLPs) and other entities also can protect assets.

None of us want to imagine our death or that of our loved ones. It is a hard and emotional topic. However, it's an important subject to bring up before an unexpected illness, accident, or death happens. At that point, the stress can be overwhelming. Do your parents, children, siblings, close friends, and yourself a favor. Open the discussion now and encourage those close to you to establish plans.

I recently interviewed Doug Paul, a managing partner of The Blum Firm, a Texas-based law firm that specializes in estate planning and wealth transfers. I was startled to learn that most individuals whom he meets for the first time have either never set up an estate plan or set one up more than five years ago. Many changes in state and federal laws have been enacted since then, and the plans were not revised accordingly.

Paul's advice? "Your estate plan should be reviewed as often as the presidential election," he says. You and your estate attorney should also pay attention to your state legislature to see if any new bills may impact your estate. It's difficult to keep up with changes in the law, but your legacy is at stake.

> **CHECKLIST**

- ⊘ *Do you have an estate plan?*
- ⊘ *Have you had it reviewed within the past four years?*
- ⊘ *Has your life drastically changed since you created your estate plan?*

PART 3

THE ALL-IMPORTANT CHECKPOINTS

10

GETTING HELP AT THE CROSSROADS

A few years ago, I stood at a personal crossroads, facing one of the hardest decisions I might ever make: Should I leave an established large corporation to join an entrepreneurial firm? The paths would lead to different life outcomes. Everything was going fine in my job. I enjoyed working for the company, liked my colleagues, and didn't have a lot of stress. However, I felt deeply that something was missing, though I couldn't figure out what it was at the time. I eventually chose to leave my job for the firm to which I still belong today.

I was fortunate to have a mentor who gave me advice I will never forget. He asked me, "What would you regret more? Making the leap and realizing you made a mistake, or never making the leap and always wondering, *What if?*"

The answer was clear to me. So, I made the leap. It didn't take long to figure out what I'd been missing. At the corporation, I was able to help people, but only within certain limits. At my current firm, I can write books, publish articles, and conduct seminars—anything to help as many people as possible. I can share the kind of planning my family needed years ago but didn't know where to get. I can help anyone at any age, demographic, or level of wealth—from teachers, policemen, and firefighters to CEOs. I love working with individuals, whether they are first-time investors or retired, to help them make sure their investments cover their goals.

Changing jobs or shifting careers is one of many checkpoints in the real game of Life. Decisions at those points are easier with the help of others—teammates, coaches, loved ones, and certainly advisors.

In the following chapters, we'll discuss some vital checkpoints and how to pass through them productively, using the financial planning tools in Part Two. Perhaps you've already gone through some of these landmark events. Think about those stages in your life. Do you have any regrets? Were there times when you sought help or a mentor? Would a life planner have helped guide you? Share your experience and knowledge of life's checkpoints with children or coworkers. Encourage them to craft a life plan, and tell them why the earlier they start living it, the better the outcome can be.

Each person has unique checkpoints. This book focuses on the ones common to most of us. While I've organized them chronologically, from the beginning of a professional career to end-of-life planning, not everyone hits these checkpoints in the same order. Some people have kids early in life; some have them later. Regardless, the arrival of a child signals an important time to stop and take stock of your plan. Whether you seek advice from a family member, a mentor, or an advisor, it's always useful to have someone help you understand your current situation and how it stacks up against your life plan.

Use these chapters as a guide to monitor and review your life plan. Are changes needed or are things on track? Let's take a look at the crucial checkpoints that signal it's time to examine your plan and find out.

CHECKLIST

- ⊘ *What major life events have occurred? What are your checkpoints?*

- ⊘ *What life events do you expect to impact your plan in the future?*

- ⊘ *Have you reviewed your plan to incorporate these events?*

11

IT'S TIME TO GROW UP

Graduating from college can be both exciting and nerve-racking. My parents used to tell me about three stages after graduation. First comes uninformed optimism. You're a college graduate and ready to impress the world. You're prepared and embarking on a career. You'll be earning your own money and able to buy anything you want!

Second is informed pessimism. You have a career, but working 40 hours a week isn't as much fun as you thought. Some of your friends still enjoy college life. You start to wonder why you jumped into the real world so quickly. Your money doesn't go as far as you thought it would. Now, you're questioning everything.

Finally, you hit the third phase of informed optimism. You enjoy your career. You have friends and relationships. Perhaps you've even learned how to budget your money to survive and actually enjoy your adult life.

My parents were joking, but their words ring true. Graduating from high school or college represents your first checkpoint and perhaps your first fork in the road. Do you go to graduate school or move into your first job? Graduate school may delay your earnings in the short run but increase your potential in the future. Can you attend graduate school part time and try to hold a job, too? It may depend on getting a scholarship or help from family. Perhaps you'll take a job with a company that provides tuition assistance for employees after a year of work. These are momentous and difficult decisions, but regardless of the outcome, you've encountered checkpoint number one.

FIRST STEPS

The moment you are responsible for yourself is the very first checkpoint in your life plan. You are suddenly a corporation of one—in charge of your own production and distribution—and it's time to take a hard look at your needs, wants, and dreams.

Before we continue, there is a phenomenon that's worth discussing—the $50,000 millionaire, which seems to have popped up everywhere. Thanks to social media and television, this is an unrealistic persona that many individuals in their 20s or 30s feel as though they need to emulate by living beyond their means.

The average starting salary for someone with a university degree is $50,000. That's great. Congratulations! You should be excited. However, that does not mean you need or can afford a brand-new Mercedes or BMW. You don't need to live in a fancy apartment by yourself. These things will come if you create a life plan and live by it. Spending freely on luxury items now, though, may mean you risk losing them quickly and will struggle to get them back later.

I love the wisdom in this quote from inspirational writer William Arthur Ward:

Work while they sleep.
Learn while they party.
Save while they spend.
Live like they dream.

I also like the saying "To live like a millionaire, you should become a millionaire!"

Until you earn your millions, though, how do you stay on track? This may be the first moment when you need a budget. It will determine how you live, and it will ensure you don't go into debt. Budgeting is an evolving process that needs to happen throughout your life and at every checkpoint.

Budgeting means remembering that you do not *need* everything you *want*. You may want access to all the available movie and TV channels, but full internet and cable can run $150 to $200 per month. With some research, you may be able to find services with similar access but lower monthly costs. You may even choose streaming services to reduce your bill. These kinds of decisions should be part of your budgeting process.

Where will you live? In early stages of a career, it's tempting to overspend on a place to live, but your rent will be a crucial part of your budget—possibly the largest part.

During my last two years of college, I lived with three roommates. Our house consisted of four bedrooms, and I was willing to take the smallest room to pay a monthly rent of just $250. Once I graduated, I moved closer to downtown and my friends' homes. I went with the cheapest apartment I could find in the vicinity, and it cost me $1,050 monthly—more than four times my college rent. I had to change my lifestyle at this point. Before, I had a lot more room in my budget. I didn't have to worry as much about eating out or enjoying activities. In my new place, I realized I had to adjust my lifestyle. I cooked more at home and looked for free activities to do with friends.

Budget for your living situation. Living with roommates is cheaper than renting by yourself. In fact, the more roommates you have, the cheaper it will be. Be realistic about what you can afford. Yes, your roommates might not be ideal. But once you find the right place, you can set ground rules. When your lease is up, you can always move.

There's one costly budget item that tends to be invisible. We don't realize that it impacts our spending because it's hard to quantify. It's called boredom, and there's actually a correlation between living alone and poor budgeting. With roommates, you have in-house companions. So, it costs less to socialize. If you want to watch sports or a movie with someone, you don't have to go to a restaurant to meet a friend. You can watch it at your place with your roommates without paying for a couple of drinks and extra food. (If you have ever watched a football game at a restaurant, you'll know what I mean.)

The other advantage to having roommates is that you have help staying on track. You can keep each other accountable. If your roommate is a friend, you can remind each other of your life plans. Did you exceed your budget for this month? Work as a team to reorganize your expenses, and get back to living your plan.

As part of the budgeting process, you need to generate cash flow and move funds into an emergency savings account as soon as you can. Start with accumulating enough to cover three months of nondiscretionary expenses—your needs. (This is just a start. See the discussion in the emergency savings section of chapter 4.) To calculate that amount, subtract all of your wants (expenses like eating out, going to the movies, and so on). Remember the pillow test? Knowing that you have enough put aside for a rainy day will let you sleep easier at night.

WHAT ABOUT WHEELS?

A new car is often our first large purchase. It can also be one of the biggest money traps. People overspend on cars all the time. I learned this the hard way when I bought my first car at age 17. I worked two jobs to save up for it and bought it as soon as I had enough. Sounds great, right? The problem is that I spent all of my savings while I lived on my own in college. I quickly realized I was stressed about paying bills. I hoped I wouldn't have any emergencies, since I didn't have extra funds.

Later, when I got my first job after graduate school, nearly everyone at my workplace drove a BMW, Mercedes, or Audi. That baffled me. I knew our salaries. How could my colleagues afford their fancy cars and expensive, uptown apartments? I couldn't help but be envious. I almost gave in and made a similar purchase, though I knew better.

During an off-site work retreat, I got to know several of my teammates. As we discussed our lives, it became clear how they bought their luxury automobiles: They sacrificed their savings and retirement funds for short-term satisfaction. "Short term" is the operative term. Twenty years later, and those same teammates now grapple with how to cover their retirement.

The takeaway of the story? Be reasonable with car purchases. An automobile—whose value declines the moment you buy it—is a tool of transportation to get you from point A to point B. Overspend on assets, not depreciating liabilities.

If you can't pay cash for your car, consider financing options. Credit unions may be a good go-to solution, but make sure their rates are competitive with other financing companies. See what a local credit union offers, then investigate the rate at a bank. There is often room to negotiate when it comes to auto loans. You may get a better rate if you have a competing offer. Anytime you can lower a rate by even a quarter point, it matters. The difference could save you $1,000 over several years, so it's worth it. Who else would hand you that?

You'll need auto insurance, too. If you purchased a new car, you'll want full coverage in case of an accident or theft. Again, make sure you shop around.

INSURANCE

As we noted, you need to have insurance, which may include policies for health, life, and disability. Begin with health insurance. If you are under the age of 26, you may be able to stay on your parents' policy. That law could change, but until it does, it may be a good option as you embark on your career.

Some employers have plans that allow a health savings account (HSA). Both you and your employer contribute to this account with pretax or tax-deductible dollars and which grow free of taxes, and you are allowed to withdraw the money tax free to pay for qualified medical expenses. Unused funds can build and be carried over from year to year. The benefit is you still have the money you built up to use for future family medical costs.

At this stage, if you're unmarried and childless, life insurance and disability insurance are unnecessary. Forgoing these premium payments means you can put that money toward savings. (If you have a family, please see the chapters on marriage and children to review your needs at those checkpoints.)

If you're living in a rented apartment, townhouse, or home, don't overlook renter's insurance, which can protect your belongings in case of a theft, flood, or other incident. Make sure to read the policy to ensure these events are covered. Where I live in Texas, many people bypassed renter's insurance and flood coverage 15 years ago. The risk of flooding seemed low, even in coastal areas. Fast-forward to today, and that situation has changed. Residents throughout the state, from Dallas and Austin to Houston, should have some kind of flood insurance. It's inexpensive in comparison to the damage that can occur, though many policies don't cover household possessions damaged by a flood or hurricane.

START SAVING NOW

It's never too early or too late to save for retirement, though it's easy to come up with excuses not to do it. People put savings on hold because they want a certain kind of house, car, or other goods and services. Thinking like that can be a mistake. Don't put off contributing toward retirement for 10 years to buy expensive season tickets for a sports team. Don't put off adding an extra $200 monthly in your 401k because you want a nice car. Don't put off contributing an extra $800 monthly because you have to buy a certain house or live in a luxury apartment. It's important to live your life, but $800 per month today can be worth $1 million in retirement if you're in your 30s or younger. Don't wait!

Income Gap & Saving Shortfall

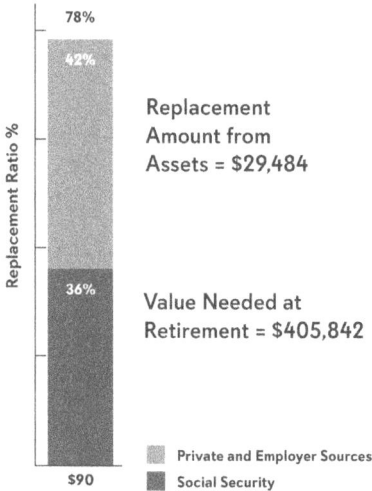

Based on a salary of $90,000 with a 78% replacement rate, assuming 30 years of contributions with a 6% annual return after fees and expenses. For illustration purposes only, **not guaranteed.** All investing involves risk.

The first step in saving for the future is to review your company's qualified retirement plan. If there is a match, contribute at least that amount. For example, a common employer match for a 401k plan is 3 percent of an employee's salary. You should contribute at least that, if not more. But I encourage any new employee to put in 6 percent of one's salary at first. If you can live off your income after that amount is subtracted, increase your contribution to 8 percent and then 10 percent. Many companies promote an IRA option over a 401k, but there are restrictions about withdrawing money from an IRA. As a young employee, it is important for you to have access to your retirement funds.

In a Roth 401k or a traditional 401k, you'll have a loan option in case anything happens: You can borrow 50 percent of the value in the fund, up to a maximum of $50,000. In a Roth IRA or traditional IRA, there is no loan option.

If you contributed the limit to your 401k or don't have a Roth option through your employer, IRAs are a good complement. The difference between a traditional IRA or 401k and the Roth versions is how they are taxed. As an individual, you contribute after-tax dollars to a Roth IRA. The gains in the Roth IRA are tax free, and any distribution that meets the requirements will be tax free. In a traditional IRA, contributions are pretax dollars. After the age of 59.5, an individual can take distributions from a traditional fund, but it will be taxed as ordinary income.

Never let the lack of an employer plan stop you from investing as early as you can. In 2019, you could contribute up to $6,000 to a traditional or Roth IRA, assuming your income was below $120,000 if you were not married. Married individuals filing jointly had a higher income limit. The figures can change each year, so be sure to check with your advisor.

As a relatively young member of the workforce, time is a gift to you. Every dollar put away now can multiply to your benefit with the power of compound interest. Start by focusing on your emergency savings, and invest that money conservatively, since it's meant to cover your needs.

Today, CDs top out at 2.4 percent and money markets at 1.5 percent. These investments are fixed, and knowing the money can't drop in value will help you pass the pillow test. Once you account for your emergency savings, you can invest in the stock and bond markets, based on your comfort with risk. The income gap analysis in the previous chart shows the power of having 40 years of savings versus 10. The earlier you contribute, the less you'll need to put away monthly to accomplish your goals.

When it comes to retirement savings, you can take more risk because your timeline is long. Don't let volatility spook you. Many individuals try to time the market or get overly involved watching their retirement account's daily or monthly performance. Don't give in to that temptation.

Dollar-cost averaging through your employee plan contributions is a strategy that balances market ups and downs. Since you purchase additional investments with every payroll, you are buying at a discount when the market drops 20 percent. As a young investor, that's what you want! The more it drops, the more you are investing at a discount—in other words, you're getting more bang for your buck. In fact, I believe you should try and contribute more when we have corrections or a bear market. It may seem counterintuitive until you run the numbers.

Notice that I didn't say try to time your investments. The point is to find a way to increase your retirement contributions when the market is down. A good rule of thumb is that when any market is down 10 percent from its highs, increase the contribution. If that stretches your budget, lower your contribution to the original percentage amount once the market recovers.

What if the market doesn't recover? Since the beginning of the stock market, it has always recovered to at least where it was before, though the timeline varies. Invest knowing this, and it will change your mindset about contributing to your 401k or IRA account.

Some easy ways exist to simplify your investments. If you are a set-it-and-forget-it type of investor, look for a target date fund in your 401k or employer-plan offerings. Target date funds are based on your retirement year goal. For example, if you plan to retire in 2040, invest in the target date fund for the year 2040. Remember, you can change the investment at any time. The benefit is that these funds are managed to the retirement year and sometimes beyond it.

The 2040 fund will have greater exposure to equities now, but closer to the retirement date, the fund will become more conservative to lower the risk of volatility. It follows a model that most investors need to know as they age with their investments. The chart that follows shows the transition of a target date fund throughout its life.

Exhibit 1: TIAA-CREF Lifecycle Funds Glidepath

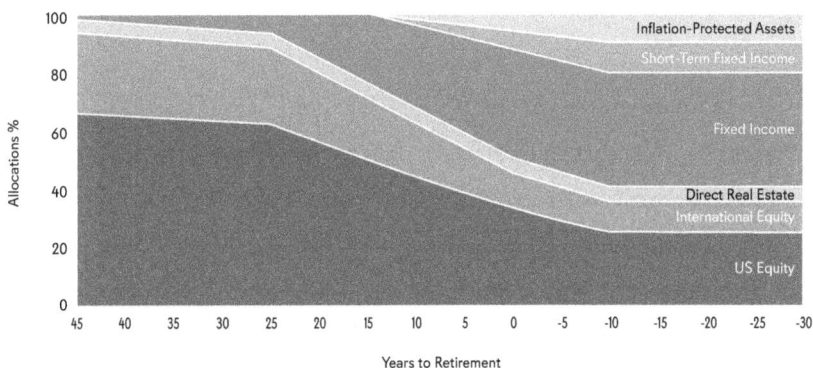

You'll notice it begins 45 years from retirement age. Almost 100 percent is invested in domestic and international equities. Once we get to 10 years past the age of retirement, the exposure has decreased to 40 percent, with the rest in fixed income.

Retirement might seem like a long way away. So how do you determine the right target date fund for you based on your age? Here's a good reference:

TIAA-CREF Target Date Funds

- ☐ TIAA-CREF Lifecycle Index Ret Inc
  - ☐ Ages 61+ (TRILX)
- ☐ TIAA-CREF Lifecycle Index 2020
  - ☐ Ages 56–60 (TRILX)
- ☐ TIAA-CREF Lifecycle Index 2025
  - ☐ Ages 51–55 (TRILX)
- ☐ TIAA-CREF Lifecycle Index 2030
  - ☐ Ages 46–50 (TRILX)
- ☐ TIAA-CREF Lifecycle Index 2035
  - ☐ Ages 41–45 (TRILX)
- ☐ TIAA-CREF Lifecycle Index 2040
  - ☐ Ages 36–40 (TRILX)

- ☐ TIAA-CREF Lifecycle Index 2045
  - ☐ Ages 31–35 (TRILX)
- ☐ TIAA-CREF Lifecycle Index 2050
  - ☐ Ages 26–30 (TRILX)
- ☐ TIAA-CREF Lifecycle Index 2055
  - ☐ Ages 25 and under (TRILX)

TIAA

As I write this book, 2060 target date funds remain available. For younger individuals just starting their careers, those may be a good base. But focus first on your target retirement year. If you know that, selecting the fund will be easier. And if you miscalculate and work three years past your goal, that's not a problem. The fund is still working for you.

INVESTING TO CLOSE THE INCOME GAP

It's commonplace to think that investing in a 401k alone will see you to retirement. If you expect high expenses, however, you probably are not saving enough to accomplish your goals, especially if you're contributing only 3 to 6 percent of your salary. We call this the income gap, and it's important to begin measuring it as soon as possible. When we meet with clients to understand their current lifestyle, it's often clear that even a goal of replacing 75 percent of their current income is impossible with their current savings.

A retirement plan should aim to close the income gap completely. If you earn $100,000 in annual compensation in the remaining years before retirement, the goal is to see if you can earn exactly $100,000 after retiring. Yes, that is undoubtedly more than you'll need, but it has a good mental effect.

In reality, the formula for calculating how much you might need is more complex because social security contributions and the Medicare tax that came out of your paycheck are gone. Contributions toward savings or retirement can also be deducted from the amount of income you'll need. Starting at the original dollar amount allows room for error, builds in some peace of mind, and incorporates wants and dreams into the goal of retirement.

CREDIT CARDS

Getting your first credit card can be an exciting moment. A company trusts you enough to give you credit, and you can borrow against it. The card may allow you to pay for your next trip with bonus points or give you cash back on your day-to-day purchases. It's an important step for anyone. I'm not here to tell you credit cards are bad. If you manage them appropriately, they can be an important tool.

But if you cannot budget, do *not* get a credit card. You have to train yourself to use a credit card in the same way you use cash. Too many individuals overspend in the belief that they will be able to pay the card off with next week's paycheck, next month's paycheck, or with a future bonus. That's the wrong attitude. You should not be paying for things now with money you expect in the future. In fact, you should be training yourself to do the opposite: saving now for purchases you expect to make. That's when you should use the benefits that credit cards can provide.

YOUR CREDIT SCORE

Credit scores have an important impact on purchases you make throughout your life, resulting in a potential difference of hundreds or thousands of dollars. Say you want to buy a new car for $25,000, and a prime rate for a car—the rate for someone with a good score of 720 or higher—is at 2.99 percent. The best subprime rate for someone with a poor credit score is 5.91 percent. That's a difference of almost 3 percent, almost double! In dollars, that comes to $449 versus $482 per month, and between $26,946 versus $28,936—a difference of close to $2,000—over a five-year loan. If that seems small, imagine the spread on a $250,000 home purchased with a 30-year loan. The number grows exponentially.

A credit score can range from 300 to 850, and ideally you want to be above 760. How do you know where you stand? First, check your current credit report with one of the three primary credit-rating agencies: Experian, Equifax, and TransUnion. That's the most important step. You can't improve your score if you don't know it. A credit score is like a GPA in college; it's a review of how you've done overall in terms of bank accounts and overall borrowing. As your borrowing changes and debts are paid, your score will improve. You can review your report for any discrepancies or issues of which you weren't aware.

Next, try to improve your score. Begin by reviewing your open credit lines. Having three different ones (two credit cards and an auto loan, for example) is a good starting point—but only if you can control your spending.

A trick to improving your credit score is to increase the limits on your credit cards. Credit bureaus analyze how much you spend compared to the funds you have available. If your monthly spending is $3,000 on a credit card with a limit of $5,000, they will see you spend 60 percent of your limit. It doesn't matter if you pay it off monthly, because they are concerned with the regular amount you are spending. Increasing the $5,000 to a $10,000 limit and maintaining the same spending lowers your borrowing percentage from 60 percent to 30 percent, which credit bureaus view in a positive light.

PETS

Before the howls start, I want to point out that I am a pet lover. I own two dogs and have owned several pets throughout my life. But when I state that the desire to have a pet is a *want* and not a *need*, I mean it. Owning a pet is costly. A dog can cost $1,000 a year. (I believe I am being conservative here; my dogs cost much more.) For someone whose take-home pay is $40,000, that represents 2.5 percent of their income. If your pet has an accident or a health issue, a one-time visit to the vet can cost $1,000. Those kinds of additional costs need to be added to your budget and accounted for in your emergency savings.

Pet insurance wasn't common when I got my first golden retriever 11 years ago, but it's now available. Consider it, and determine if it fits into your budget.

When it comes to wants, pets may be a priority, but please understand the associated costs before making a hasty decision. The worst-case scenario is getting a pet and having to give it up later.

CHECKLIST

- ✓ *Are you successfully living on a budget?*
- ✓ *Are you planning and managing your debt?*
- ✓ *Have you updated your emergency fund?*
- ✓ *Do you know your credit score?*
- ✓ *Are you managing your credit cards appropriately?*
- ✓ *Are you saving and investing?*

12

MARRIAGE

My wife and I vacationed with her parents recently. My father-in-law joked that he still doesn't know how much our wedding cost. My mother-in-law responded, "You never will!"

Marriage is an important checkpoint in most of our lives. Now two of you are making decisions, and, as my in-laws correctly noted, the act of getting married itself can be expensive, beginning with the engagement. One of the first things people tell me when they find out I have two daughters, with another on the way, is that now I'll have to pay for three weddings!

Budgeting for a wedding may be one of the very first joint financial decisions a couple makes, and it's easy to get carried away by the romance of the occasion. My own wedding was amazing. My wife and I enjoyed every moment of it. With hindsight, we might have done things a little differently. A wedding goes by in a matter of hours, and it can take hundreds of hours of planning and cost thousands to tens of thousands of dollars. Moreover, it's not the wedding that makes the marriage successful. That depends on love, and it's easier to love each other in the absence of financial stress.

That brings us back to budgeting, which, as I've noted before, comes into play at each checkpoint. With two of you, the psychology of your relationship plays a role in figuring out how to spend your money. My wife is an emotional person through and through. In contrast, I am extremely analytical. That means we may bicker about our budget. We joke that her purchases are emotional and mine are mostly rational, though we all make emotional purchases at one time or another. Despite our differences, my wife and I work extremely well together using a 48-hour rule. Before buying something, we give ourselves 48 hours to sleep on it and decide if we really need the item.

I have seen many marriages struggle with budgeting because the partners avoid addressing how differently each of them looks at financial matters. Understand this, and it will make it easier to budget with a partner.

Budgeting may even be easier when two working adults marry, since two incomes are involved. You and your spouse also will have two sets of expenses to review, however, and you'll need to understand each other's debts and priorities. Ideally, these issues are discussed *before* the wedding. The goal is to begin marriage on the same page and with a joint plan. From this point on, Life is a team game.

To begin with, a married couple living together should have fewer expenses if they're both employed. Take rent, for example. Whether you are renting a place or have purchased a home, you've gone from two payments to one. If your previous rents each totaled $1,000 a month, you have now saved $12,000 a year! Don't rush to spend it all at once. Instead, plan to put some of this into savings to build your life together. Aim for 50 percent in savings, then try to use some of the remaining 50 percent to pay down debts. The remainder can finance a trip or a regular date night.

It's important to ask about your spouse's needs, wants, and dreams. Discuss how these align with yours. Sit down and review them. The needs that are the same for both of you will be your true needs. Seek your advisor's help if you need it. The discussion should not begin an argument; it's a healthy conversation about the future. As I said, Life is now a team game for you, and teammates debate all the time. They do it because they want to win together. They care about a game or a championship. Your life plan together should have the same effect. Each day, week, month, and year, you are both contributing to the team to ensure that you are winning.

Review your emergency savings and consider your pillow test. The amount you set aside may need to be increased since in an emergency there would be expenses for both of you.

Discuss your retirement-planning objectives. Who has the best employer retirement plan? What is the optimal way to put away the funds needed for retirement? If you cannot afford as a couple to contribute enough to maximize an employer match, the spouse with the highest income—and presumably the highest match—should contribute as much as possible. That's like adding free money to your plan. It's the easiest step to take, especially if one spouse isn't taking advantage of an employer match.

Many newly married couples rush to begin a family. That's an important life decision. You and your spouse may decide to build a life together first. These early years are your best opportunity to get ahead in your life and financial plan. The more you can accomplish toward your goals now, the better you can take advantage of our good friend: time.

If you're both still young, don't rush to buy a house or even upgrade to a luxury apartment if you can manage more modest accommodations for a while. If you buy a house, try not to over-reach. The time for your dream home is not early in your career; it should be easier to achieve later. Purchase a home that you can view as an investment and a place to live. That might mean a home that you can rent out when you are ready to move up to more luxurious quarters. I challenge you to view your home as an asset.

Now that you're married, estate planning also may be new to you. Many individuals wait too long to update beneficiaries on their investments and retirement funds, for example. If you have an IRA or employer retirement plans such as a 401k, add your spouse as your beneficiary. Others designate their estate. Do not leave the beneficiary space blank! Having a spouse on the account will allow it to be transferred to your spouse's name automatically without entering the judicial process of probate. It's also important to create a basic will in case something were to happen. This will allow any court to follow instructions based on your estate plan.

Review the coverage on your auto insurance and add each other to all policies, regardless of who drives the most. It's rare that you and your spouse will have identical insurance coverage. Review your plans to see which is best for you as a married couple.

Marriage is one of the biggest decisions we make in life, if not *the* biggest. After all, this is the person with whom you choose to live the rest of your life. Even before the wedding, it helps to understand each other's finances and make sure you communicate well. Why? Finances and a lack of communication are two of the leading causes of divorce.

THE SECOND—OR THIRD—TIME AROUND

Remarriage is as common as divorce, and it's another important checkpoint. On the one hand, both parties may have progressed in their careers and earn higher incomes. On the other hand, the blending of families may lead to more expenses.

No matter your situation, a new relationship involves budgeting once again. What are your individual expenses and incomes? It's important to understand each other's needs, wants, and dreams. Are you in a strong situation to achieve them together, or do you need to make some adjustments?

With remarriage, estate planning is crucial and tends to be more complex, especially if children from a previous relationship or marriage are involved. The laws governing estate planning and remarriage, which are subject to change, are also more complicated and can vary from state to state. It's important to protect your interests. If your goal is to give part of the estate to your children outside of the new marriage, an estate plan *must* be created and discussed before the wedding or soon after.

For instance, take Madeline and her husband, John, who were very happy together. It was a second marriage for John, who had children from a prior relationship. Those children, now adults, had frequent disputes with Madeline. They just couldn't seem to get along. John had not done any estate planning, and when he passed, his estate went to probate.

He and Madeline had a house in both of their names, and state laws held John's portion of the house should go to his children. They now owned 50 percent of the house where Madeline lived, and the relationship worsened. After months of bickering, she was emotionally drained and chose to sell the house, taking her share of the proceeds. A simple estate plan for John could have ensured that Madeline would own and stay in their home.

Asset protection is a common part of estate planning after a second marriage. If you have been successful in your career or have a lot of savings, the thought of losing half that money or more in a second divorce is daunting.

Tax planning is unique to couples. One of you may have to provide support to a previous spouse through alimony, child support, or a court-ruled payment. With your advisor, investigate ways to deduct some of these payments. Gifting can also be a valuable strategy and a way to provide your children with funds while protecting your assets.

CHECKLIST

- ✓ *Do you and your spouse work on your budget together?*
- ✓ *Have you updated your emergency fund?*
- ✓ *Have you revisited your debt, insurance, and investments together?*
- ✓ *Have you reviewed your tax planning because of any life changes?*
- ✓ *Have you done an estate plan?*
- ✓ *Do you have a will?*

13

PURCHASING A HOME

For many investors, a home is the largest purchase they will make in their lifetime. I grew up believing this was one of the biggest things to accomplish as an adult. It's exciting. The first opportunity I had to buy a home, I went out and bought one. I was 26 years old at the time.

Less than one year later, I was offered a job in a different state that I couldn't pass up. Unfortunately, the house sold for the same price I paid for it, minus the closing costs, which included realtors' commissions of 6 percent—3 percent for the buying agent and 3 percent for the selling agent. I ended up losing money on the sale.

Many of us believe that a home is one of the best possible investments we can make. As with any major checkpoint, it's important to review every aspect of our life plan before we run out to find the house of our dreams. Real estate bubbles occur, wreaking havoc on finances if we've stretched our budget to the breaking point or used some form of complex financing. Before you buy a house, go through this checkpoint and review all the numbers.

Examine your budget. How much can you afford if you transition your rent into a mortgage, tax, and insurance payment? That is an ideal scenario and the easiest way to maintain your budget while purchasing a home. The only better option is if your house payment is lower than your rent.

For many of us, however, the payment will be higher. What we can control is how much higher. Do we *need* an ultra-large home? Remember the discussion about needs, wants, and dreams? See how those concepts apply to your situation. Work with your budget. Work with your spouse if you're married. Figure out what you need now and what you'll need if you have a family. Strive to fulfill your wants, but realize paying for a home can be very stressful if you overreach.

Most of us have either owned real estate or considered purchasing real estate at some point in our lifetimes. Is it an investment or not? Is it the only investment we need? Our answers may not all be the same, but they should be taken into account at this checkpoint in our life plan.

In this chapter, our focus will be on single-family purchases and the associated costs.

First, it's important to understand that there's more to a home purchase than the list price. Closing costs when you purchase a home can run 1 to 2 percent and can cost you 6 to 8 percent on the sale. If an investor were shopping for a market investment and an advisor proposed one that charged these same costs, the investor would laugh and move on. Yet many individuals jump into these types of real estate investments assuming that they cannot lose. In fact, on the low end in this example, a home price would have to increase by 7 percent to break even. If you have to move before the home has appreciated to that extent, you could be forced to take a loss or rent it out.

Don't forget about property taxes, either. In Texas, property taxes hover around 3 percent annually. If an investment manager charged 3 percent annually, you'd walk away.

It's true that a client who owns a home can build equity through mortgage payments, but it takes time. At first, most of a mortgage payment will go toward paying interest. Only a little will actually go to reducing principal.

Let's take a look at an example. An investor buys a home for $250,000 and puts down 20 percent. The home buyer intends to pay off the $200,000 mortgage over 30 years. The total principal paid will be $200,000, but the interest will amount to about $165,000 over the same time. Total cost? A surprising $365,000.

$ 250,000	

Down payment

$ 50,000	20.00 %

Mortgage term

30 years	360 months

Annual interest rate

4.5 %	CALCULATE

Your estimated monthly payment:

$1,013.37

Total principal paid	$200,000.00
Total interest paid	$164,813.42

Bankrate Calculator

In the same example, the amortization table shows that out of the first payment of $1,013, $750 of it goes toward interest. The remaining amount is principal. It will take 15 years for the principal and interest to balance out. After that point, the principal paid exceeds the interest.

Start Date

08/18/2018

Estimated Payoff Date

August 18, 2048

Amortization Schedule

Payment Date	Payment	Principal	Interest	Total Interest	Balance
Sep 2018	$1,013.37	$263.37	$750.00	$750.00	$199,736.63
Oct 2018	$1,013.37	$264.36	$749.01	$1,499.01	$199,472.27
Nov 2018	$1,013.37	$265.35	$748.02	$2,247.03	$199,206.92
Dec 2018	$1,013.37	$266.34	$747.03	$2,994.06	$198,940.58

Before you buy a house, try to negotiate the mortgage interest rate. Shop around and read the small print and every disclosure in any agreement. Perhaps you see an attractive rate, but it's only for those with a high credit score, or it may depend on a huge down payment.

Don't neglect homeowner's insurance. Review the options available to you, and make sure you've covered at least the amount of the loan. Ideally, your insurance will cover the full purchase price, not just the loan value. Shop around for the best policy.

Lines of credit may come in handy if you're buying a new home before your old home is sold. A bridge loan may be more useful than liquidating a portfolio and paying taxes on gains to cover some of the home buying costs.

Know your liability for fees in the future. At some point, if you intend to sell a house using a realtor, you'll pay a commission. In Texas, you'll be looking at commission expenses of 6 percent plus closing costs. (You could choose to sell the home without a realtor, which would eliminate the commission.)

Or, instead of selling the house, you could rent it out. You'll encounter fees here, too, especially if you outsource the property management. Since property management companies may have a wide range of fees, it's important for you to shop around and learn what costs are involved.

Payment Date	Payment	Principal	Interest	Total Interest	Balance
Mar 2033	$1,013.37	$505.14	$508.23	$112,362.04	$135,022.18
Apr 2033	$1,013.37	$507.04	$506.33	$112,868.37	$134,515.14
May 2033	$1,013.37	$508.94	$504.43	$113,372.81	$134,006.21
Jun 2033	$1,013.37	$510.85	$502.52	$113,875.33	$133,495.36

Bank Rate Calculator

Let's compare funds spent on a house to other kinds of investments. Assume you invested $50,000 by making monthly contributions of $1,013.37. If you earned a conservative return of 3 percent on the investments, the value would be $713,155 before taxes. Can real estate properties grow this much in value? Absolutely! Areas of the country have outpaced this rate over 30 years, while other areas have done drastically worse.

Now let's imagine the rate of return on your investment is 8 percent, which is roughly the average of the S&P 500 over the past 100 years. The total amount earned after 30 years is $2,056,521 before taxes. You'd have an 800 percent return from the original amount invested!

Your current plan produces $713,155 after 30 years before taxes and inflation.

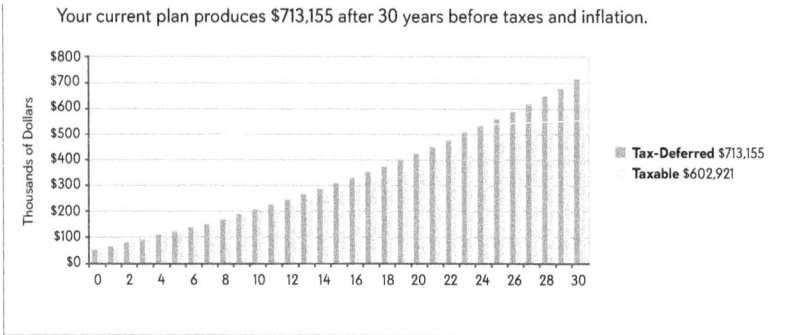

What can we take away from these comparisons? People need a place to live, but they also should save for retirement. There needs to be a reasonable balance between these goals, but most individuals lean toward paying more for a home than saving for retirement. They hope their home will be their retirement nest egg when they sell it, but some problems arise with this train of thought.

The first problem is you still need a place to live. That will cost you something in rent or mortgage payments, so you won't be investing and living off of the full value of the home you sold. The second problem is you'll face closing costs in a home sale, plus the taxes on any gains. If you are going to view it as a nest egg, you need to lower the value after closing costs and taxes to get a good grasp of its true value going forward. Use this true value in your financial plan.

It's easy to be seduced into buying a house you can't really afford. You may see friends or family living in large homes and want one too. That desire forces many people to overreach and pay a mortgage well above their recommended income levels. One rule of thumb is not to exceed more than 36 percent of your gross income. A great goal is 25 percent. Anything lower is phenomenal.

CHECKLIST

- ✓ *Have you planned for your home purchase?*

- ✓ *Have you budgeted appropriately for the payments?*

- ✓ *Are your insurance and estate plans updated to include the house?*

14

CHILDREN

My wife and I married in our mid-20s. We were young, but we knew we wanted to spend our lives together. Like many newlyweds, we had expectations of traveling, building a nest, and preparing for a family. Shortly after marriage, however, I was offered a career opportunity that would take us 1,000 miles away from family and friends. It opened a new, exciting chapter for us, one in which we would have to depend on each other closely.

Shortly after the move, we sat down and planned out the next three years. We thought we'd both focus on our careers and on us. We'd revisit the idea of children later. You may have realized by now that I analyze everything and try to plan as much as possible. Little did we know, while we spent the weekend mapping out our lives, my wife was already pregnant with our first daughter.

I don't care how much you plan, those expectations will change when it comes to children. That's okay; it's part of the fun of life. It's why plans adapt, evolve, and need to be constantly reviewed.

Children are the biggest checkpoint in many of our lives. The responsibilities of our team have increased, and so has the complexity. I have two children whom I love, and I can't imagine life without them. However, their arrival came with a lot of financial stress since my wife chose to quit work and stay home. We were not as prepared for that as we could have been. Now we're expecting a third girl and have a much better plan. Finances are not stressful for us because we have been able to use our experience to plan and prepare.

All new parents have to make big decisions. For example, one parent may choose not to work outside the home, which results in sacrificing income and creating a big budgetary shift. Alternatively, both parents may continue to work. In that case, you'll likely need day care, but it doesn't come cheap. When we looked at day care in Austin, Texas, the cost ran to about $1,500 monthly. This comes out to $25,000 in gross income. If your household brings in $80,000 total, you are giving up 31.25 percent of your gross income. That doesn't include diapers, food, clothes, and other necessities for a child. The impact can be dramatic if you haven't planned for it.

The answer? You guessed it, budgeting. Children can be an expensive add-on to a household. They also may affect your flexibility in many ways, including how you manage your time. At one point, you might have gone into work later, earlier, or even worked weekends, but now you have other demands on your time.

In our case, when my wife and I both worked, we had to pick up our children by 5:30 p.m. from day care. If we didn't make this deadline, we had to pay a penalty of $50. We both had demanding jobs at the time. To balance things, we decided that one of us could go in earlier to take the kids to school and pick them up. Even that was difficult and caused us stress. Eventually, both for financial reasons and to accommodate my wife's desire to spend more time with our children, it made more sense for her to stay home and for me to work more to make up for the lost income.

Your emergency savings have to be increased to account for any additions to your family. Insurance coverage also needs to be reviewed. This is the time, too, to consider life insurance to protect the family in case anything happens to you or your partner. Whether both parents are working or just one, you need to have life insurance for both of you.

Some companies may provide life insurance for their employees, but usually it is capped at an amount less than a family may need. Supplemental employer policies for a spouse usually are even less adequate. Keep in mind, too, that employer policies will not go with you if you change jobs. This is why every parent needs to look at an independent term policy. These are affordable, and you can get a large policy for a reasonable contribution. As we noted before, a term policy means the insurance policy has a maturity date. A 20-year term policy started today means the policy would end in 20 years if nothing happened. Since the policy expires if it isn't used, it's affordable for a large death benefit.

Disability insurance also becomes important at this time, especially if one spouse decides to stay at home or decrease their workload. It's crucial to protect the main provider's income. The costs for disability insurance are often cheaper through one's employer, but review the coverage and costs before signing. If you're in a career where employees change jobs frequently, look for independent coverage that can travel with you when you move to a different job. This way, you won't have a lapse in coverage.

Your estate plan needs to be updated when you add children (new beneficiaries) to your life. It's important to formally add them to your will and other assets to create a smoother estate-planning process in case anything were to happen to your spouse and you at the same time. It's a scary thought but one for which you should always plan.

If college tuition for your children is an important part of your plan, start as soon as possible. Keeping up with rising tuition costs can only be done if you begin saving early. As a parent, the earlier you contribute toward college savings for your children, the more likely you are to have money to assist your children with tuition. Alternatively, you may prefer that your children take loans for tuition. Make sure you and your spouse agree about your course of action even before the birth of your first child, because the time frame for education savings is shorter than your time frame for retirement.

No matter your age, you have various options for college funds. One program, called a Coverdell ESA, allows you to make an annual contribution of $2,000 and has flexibility for how you can use the funds. A so-called 529 plan allows you to contribute up to $15,000 annually, or you can do a five-year lump-sum contribution of $75,000. This is attractive for individuals who have kids later in life and already have money saved. The lump-sum contribution can also help you offset income for taxes.

As I've noted earlier, it's not a good idea to let planning for college interfere with saving for your own retirement. Keep up your employee match in any IRA or 401k plan. You probably won't be able to increase your contribution, but remember the match is free money your employer contributes to your retirement plan. If you have been able to build up your contributions, try to maintain your current rate. Challenge yourself not to have to lower it.

Having children raises new questions when it comes to tax planning. You'll have an additional dependent or dependents, which may lower the withholding from your paycheck if you decide to claim them. In general, your tax situation will become more complex, so you may want to work with an advisor to help you understand the changes. You can decide not to add the dependent on your W-4 and hope for a decent-size tax refund, but you need to weigh both options.

We discussed itemizing in the tax-planning section. It's important to understand the difference between standard deductions and itemizing on your annual tax forms. The more expenses that are deductible, the more likely you can itemize. Different IRA types, education accounts, and other investments can help you defer or lower your taxable income if you itemize. These become important the more you earn and the more you try to invest toward achieving long-term goals.

Your health insurance costs will rise when you have children. In my case, the costs actually doubled when I added kids to my plan. When it comes to a budget, health insurance is a need that should be part of your savings each year. If you have a health savings account (HSA), your deductible will be higher than for a non-HSA option.

An HSA is a tax-deferred account to which you can contribute. The account can grow year over year and can be invested. When you have a medical situation, you can use the funds tax free to pay the expenses. You need to determine if this is still the best option because early childhood can be expensive and the policies tend to have a higher deductible. An example is a $7,500 deductible compared to a lower deductible of $5,000 without an HSA that can take contributions. Look at the options with a low deductible and maximum out-of-pocket expenses.

In some lower-deductible plans, a flexible spending account (FSA) is available. You can achieve the same tax benefits as the HSA but with a lower deductible amount. The major difference between an HSA and an FSA is that an HSA can be built up, whereas any unused funds in an FSA will be lost at year's end.

In the early stages of childhood, doctor visits are frequent, and costs will escalate. For a first-time parent, a baby's first year may bring many scares. Any sign of illness could lead to emergency visits and medical expenses. It is the rare parent who doesn't go through their whole deductible in the first years of parenting.

For example, if your deductible for the year is $5,000 and maximum out of pocket is $10,000, you want to make sure you have this amount saved. The likelihood of medical or emergency visits with children is higher than when it was just you and your spouse. If you don't have this savings, $10,000 can be a lot to finance and pay back. Any major injury or illness is less likely to set you back if you can afford your maximum out-of-pocket costs.

Having children is not just a one-time checkpoint. You have to go through these decisions every time you add a new dependent to your life. As your family grows, so will your expenses. Your budget will change, your estate plan will change, and your health insurance will be more expensive. These decisions also may evolve as your children get older, as we'll see in the following sections.

My goal is to emphasize the importance of planning before every important step in your life. Having children is a major decision that can affect you financially. With a life plan, you will sleep better at night, even if you have to wake up six times to feed and change the baby.

CHILDREN IN HIGH SCHOOL

By the time your children are in high school, new decisions are in order. For instance, you have to decide if you'll allow them to drive your car after they pass their driver's test and get a license. In any case, they will need to be added to all auto insurance policies.

It's also time to consider if they will get their own car and whether you'll purchase it for them, which becomes another budget item. Consider giving them a used car so they can get used to driving (and you can get used to their driving too!). If you've budgeted for a nicer or new car for your child, consider saving that purchase for when he or she is older. Consider it a want, not a need.

As parents, we often work hard to provide our kids with the same or better life opportunities. I've seen individuals put their retirement or other goals on hold to provide their children with cars and other material possessions.

Last year, I met with some longtime clients. They have four children, three girls and one boy ranging in age from seventh grade to senior year in high school. They had reached another checkpoint because some of their kids were about to attend college. We sat down to revisit their plan.

This was a stressful time for them. They knew their life was going to go through a major shift. From a financial standpoint, their expenses should have been decreasing and their savings increasing. They had bought new cars for their oldest two kids and wanted to take out a large withdrawal to purchase one for their third child.

"Why a new car?" I asked. They responded that the parents at their kids' school always purchased new cars for their children. They didn't want their kid to be judged. I asked how the new cars had gone for the first two children. They laughed as they told me that both kids had wrecks within the first year. Not terrible wrecks, but enough to do damage and incur hefty expenses. At this point, they had spent $60,000 and were going to spend another $30,000 on automobiles for their children rather than invest these considerable funds in their own retirement.

KIDS IN COLLEGE

The decisions you make about your children and college have a huge impact on your life. I recently met with new clients Dave and Susan, who are in their late 50s and trying to determine when and if they can retire. Their four children are grown and independent. Susan had not been employed outside the home, but Dave's income was $350,000 annually. He had significant earnings for the past 20 years, and the couple was 10 years away from retirement. Dave had contributed up to his employer's match in his retirement plan but added nothing more.

I asked how they had spent most of their earnings to have saved so little. Susan explained they had invested in their children to give them opportunities they never had. They had paid roughly $15,000 annually for each child to attend private school throughout kindergarten and high school, then paid for college tuition as well—which averaged $25,000 a year. Two of the children had gone to graduate school. Then there were the usual fun items such as eating out, family vacations, and other memorable moments.

Decisions about public versus private school are the province of each individual family. But it's worthwhile to look at the impact on Dave and Sue's finances. Had the kids gone to public schools and the family invested the $15,000 tuition a year over 13 years—times four—with a conservative return of 3 percent annually, they would have saved $965,179 based on private school tuition alone.

As for college tuition, let's say each child graduates in four years and can fully support themselves. Using the same assumption of a 3 percent return, the money invested instead of paid as tuition would be worth about $431,000. Adding college and private school together results in a total of nearly $1.4 million.

Had Dave and Susan sent their kids to public school instead of private, they would have been able to retire the day we sat down together. Instead they needed a million dollars more for retirement, which would take time and strict budgeting on their part.

Another risk to putting funds in college savings accounts is that your children may not go to college. Few of us want to believe this is a possibility, but odds say it is a real one.

If you are adamant about a college savings account, research the different types that are available, including Coverdells, 529 plans, and plans based on the Uniform Gift Minors Act or Uniform Transfer to Minors Act (UGMA/UTMA, depending on the state). Each account has its own purpose and rules on whether you have to use the funds specifically for college. They also have different contribution limits and advantages.

The 529 and Coverdell plans have tax benefits and are used specifically for educational expenses. Withdrawing funds from 529 plans for anything other than higher education can result in a penalty and taxes. They also have different contribution limits and may have a few different rules on required usage.

UGMA/UTMA accounts are used to put money aside for a child until they reach the age of "maturity." (The exact age and definition depends on the state in which the account is set up.) For these funds, there is no limitation or penalty on usage of funds. However, you lose the tax benefit.

Another option is to build up a taxable investment account and use this to pay tuition. There are no tax deductions with this method, but you have the ability to be flexible with the funds. You can use it for expenses other than direct college expenses. Also, if your child gets a scholarship or doesn't end up going to college, you are not penalized.

When your children enter college, you have a chance to teach them how to budget and live on their own. I encourage you to take advantage of this learning opportunity. If you are not ahead of your retirement goals, do not abandon them to pay for college. Many options exist for a college education, including scholarships and loans. Compare the costs of state or public universities to private school tuition. Public universities can be less than half the cost of a private institution.

In November 2018, CNBC writer Abigail Hess wrote about universities that have produced the most current Fortune 500 CEOs and found that top public schools had the same number as their Ivy League competition. She also compared their tuition, which was more than $50,000 for the Ivy League and, in some cases, less than $20,000 for state schools. That's a difference worth taking into account.

Sometimes our kids specialize in an area that calls for an advanced degree. In that case, you'll have to determine if they need a loan or if you can afford the additional costs. I like to joke that you should always plan for a master's degree and settle for a PhD, since statistics show that the highest levels of education pay off in terms of future salaries.

Benjamin Franklin once stated, "An investment in knowledge pays the best interest." If your child's goal is to become a doctor or lawyer, don't scratch the dream because of costs, but try to control them through the choice of school they attend and the tuition you pay.

> **CHECKLIST**

- ⊘ *Have you updated your budget?*
- ⊘ *Have you updated your emergency savings, estate plan, tax plan, and insurance?*
- ⊘ *Does your health-care plan fit your family situation?*
- ⊘ *Are you putting retirement before your child's college education?*

15

THE PRIME OF YOUR LIFE

Once the kids have left home, your expenses should be lower. Then you can begin to picture retirement life. Your household is probably down to just you and your spouse with maybe a couple of pets. You are now at a place where you need to revisit your plan, adjust your budget, and use your current expenses as a real-life example of what to expect in the future. Review your retirement plan to determine how far or close you are to achieving your goals. Do you need to save more, or are you doing well enough that your funds will carry you through? It's important to revisit your wants and dreams in retirement. They may be very different now that your children are self-sufficient and you're closer to your goals.

I know from personal experience how wants and dreams change throughout our lives. Ours have evolved in the past four years since my wife and I have had children. We used to think of retiring in a nice home with all the amenities. Now we realize we love being out of the house more than in it. We're hoping someday to live in a city in a two-bedroom condo or an apartment where almost everything is done for us—a place where we can pack up, leave at a moment's notice, and not have to worry about who is taking care of things while we are gone. I can only imagine how much our goals will have changed again 16 years from now.

CHANGING JOBS

Careers are not static. In the past, individuals may have worked almost their entire lives for one company, even at the same job. That is no longer true. Career changes or milestones are another kind of checkpoint at which to reconsider your needs, wants, and dreams to reevaluate your life plan.

I've heard it said that companies will pay more to recruit you than to keep you. A job offer may be tempting, but it's important to ask some questions before you make a jump to another company. Two things to consider—

- Will you need to move, and are the costs covered?
- Are you leaving money on the table?

Moving from one state to another can run into the tens of thousands of dollars if you have a family and own a home. The opportunity may be incredible, but be sure you add moving costs to the picture to see if it still is monetarily worth it.

Since I was 17, the longest I have lived in one place was two years. I know the cost of moving and how it can add up over time if you frequently relocate. If your career calls for multiple moves, don't overspend on items like furniture, which can be ruined and limit your flexibility. The same salary that lets you afford a four-bedroom home in Fort Worth, Texas, might only pay for a much smaller space in San Francisco, California, with no room for that oversized couch.

Before accepting a job with a new company, make sure you also measure what you are leaving on the table. For example, you may have a 401k with a five-year vesting period. If you are close to an anniversary, a portion of your company match may vest. This is money you can take with you if you wait until your anniversary to change jobs. Similarly, your old company may have restricted stock with a vesting period. If you have to forgo funds with a job change, you may be able to negotiate the amount you are leaving on the table as a signing bonus or added incentive to join the new company.

You need to review your future company's retirement benefits as well. Do they offer a 401k, and what is the vesting period? Is there an opportunity to earn or purchase stock at a discount? Will they offer an HSA or an FSA? Is there a health and wellness benefit, in which a company credits you a certain amount of money for being healthy? All these benefits should factor into your decision and your planning for the future.

GETTING TO $1 MILLION

It's true the first million is the hardest to earn. Once you get to this level, it's time to pause and pat yourself on the back. Why is the first million so difficult? Budgeting, investments, and poor life decisions all play a role, among other factors. But if your assets add up, $1 million invested can continue to increase more quickly:

A nine-year period with an 8 percent return will double your investment.

This financial landmark is another checkpoint. Begin by reviewing your insurance coverage. So-called umbrella coverage can increase your protection up to $1 million and more in assets. It can protect you against future liabilities, such as a car wreck that is your fault. Your advisor can help you shop for coverage with your current carriers or help you find a new one.

If, up to this point, your estate plan was just a basic will or simply your 401k, it's time to consider additional asset protection. A trust, for example, may be a fit for some people as their estate grows.

RETIREMENT PLANNING

This is one of the last checkpoints we all face. Once again, budgeting is the first step. It's tempting to envision a lavish lifestyle when we retire. However, most of us will find we have an income gap because we haven't saved enough. Be hard-nosed about which expenses you'll be willing to pay in retirement and which ones can be phased out. The lower your expenses, the greater the probability you will achieve your wants and dreams.

Next, analyze your cash flow to see if you can live off the return on your investments without digging into principal. The goal is to ensure the principal doesn't run out before your death. As a planner, I always use worst-case assumptions and lower expected rates of return in making any analysis of future cash flow. The higher the probability of success using the lowest assumptions helps the client—and me—sleep at night.

As if saving money for retirement weren't daunting enough, there are other potential pitfalls. You may have a strict budget and know your cash flow. However, you've still got to watch out for boredom, health care, auto insurance, inflation, and fees. Once you know they're coming and have planned for them, you can expect smooth sailing on your journey to retirement.

Boredom

Have you ever caught yourself online shopping only because you were bored? There's a "browse" option on Amazon for a reason. The company has made spending money so easy that all it takes is a few clicks. Think about your weekends, too. If you're bored, the natural inclination is to go to a movie, go out to eat, go to a game, and so on. Imagine you're retired, and you've suddenly got 40 or more hours of free time every week that you never had before. What will you do while you're sitting around the house? Planning is more important than ever. What will your hobbies be? Will you volunteer? Work part time? It's crucial to keep yourself occupied, even in retirement, so that you make the most of your retirement savings.

Health Care

Advances in health care can sometimes translate to increased expenses. Medicare won't always cover 100 percent of medical expenses. Retiree health premiums also are rising dramatically. If your health worsens, a good chunk of your retirement income could go toward medical expenses. Depending on your retirement age, you may not qualify for Medicare. Here are a few professional tips:

- Get a health savings account (HSA). Both contributions and payouts are tax free. Contributions can lower your gross income, potentially putting you in a lower tax bracket. These accounts, which are designed to be spent only on your health needs, also carry over year after year. If you've been putting money into an HSA for 20 years, chances are your balance is very high. You can use that money for all your medical expenses in retirement, tax free.

- Understand your health insurance. Read the fine print on your policy.

- Because people are living much longer, the demand for long-term care has increased. However, long-term care policies can be complicated and expensive. You may die before ever using the policy and lose all of the premiums you paid into it. The good thing is that more products are becoming available. Some policies provide a death benefit *and* long-term care insurance. Thus, your beneficiaries won't lose all that you paid into it. Contact an advisor if you think you might need some help. Carefully read the prospectus before signing any agreements.

Auto Insurance

This is an issue that isn't as important as health care, but it still requires review at checkpoints. Full coverage becomes crucial because you want to protect your family from the costs of a car wreck and associated medical costs, especially as your net worth increases. Here's an example: Perhaps you have a child in high school who was texting, driving, and at fault in a collision. The victim could hire a lawyer and come after your insurance and even personal assets that are not protected. That is why you want to increase the coverage as your family grows and as you age.

Inflation

A dollar today doesn't equal a dollar tomorrow. Just for fun, here's a quick look at the history of a loaf of bread: In 1930, a loaf cost $0.09; in 1970, $0.70; in 2013, it cost $1.98. Inflation is as certain as death and taxes. You've got to plan ahead for it. If you think you'll retire in 20 years, consider how inflation might impact the amount you need.

Reduction of Purchasing Power over Time

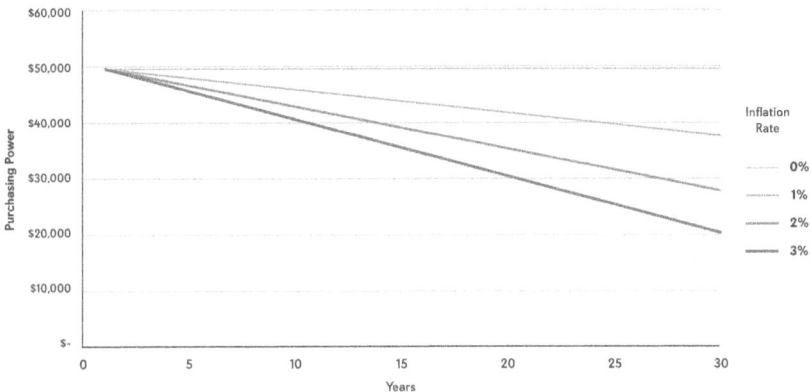

During our working years, we invest our retirement funds to account for inflation. But what about after work is over? If you plan to enjoy retirement for 20-plus years, the money you've saved probably won't keep up with the rise in the cost of living. Keep these tips in mind as you make your investments:

- Invest in portfolios that are meant to outpace inflation.
- Use a higher inflation number to provide yourself a cushion in your plan.
- Add some investments correlated with inflation.
- Save more early on.

Fees

Fees are crafty little villains. If you're investing your retirement savings, it's vital that you understand your account fees. If you're not paying attention, you could be losing 5 percent or more. Here's a quick visual to illustrate the point:

The Fee Effect

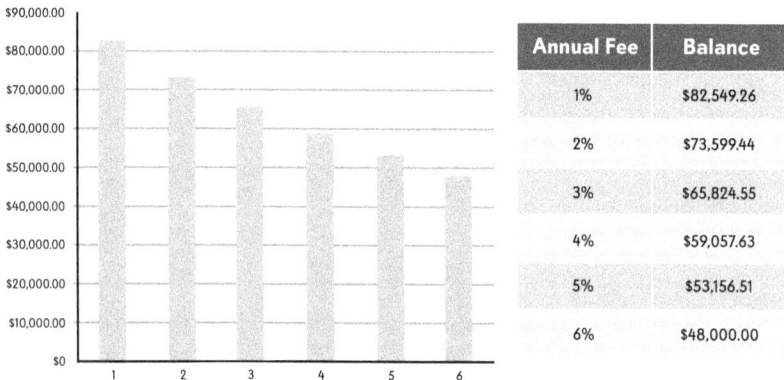

Annual Fee	Balance
1%	$82,549.26
2%	$73,599.44
3%	$65,824.55
4%	$59,057.63
5%	$53,156.51
6%	$48,000.00

Balance based on 6% earning net of fees with $200 monthly contributions for 20 years at the beginning of the month.
Actual rate of return is **not guaranteed**. For illustrations purposes only. All investing involves risk.

Notice how quickly the fees add up. The difference between 1 percent and 2 percent in annual fees for a $200 contribution over 20 years is a difference of 12.2 percent in cumulative growth. If you need help identifying your account fees, don't hesitate to reach out to an advisor.

Medicare

When we reach age 65, Medicare is an option that many of us depend on for health care, but laws are constantly changing. The options are complex and not easy to interpret, but these decisions will impact you financially for the rest of your life.

Choosing the right option on your own can be daunting. For example, does it make sense to get a policy that provides full coverage, or lesser coverage with a supplemental policy? Anytime you have more than a couple of options, it can be difficult to decide which is best. Make it more than 10 options and paralysis by analysis becomes real. Many retirees feel alone in this decision, but an advisor may be able to guide them.

Another issue is what to do if you decide to retire before 65 or continue to work beyond that age? Options available through the Affordable Care Act can help you obtain health-care coverage if you plan to retire before age 65. If you plan to work past 65, don't rush to join Medicare. Your corporate coverage may be cheaper and provide a better benefit to your family and you.

CHECKLIST

- *Do you have a goal of paying off all your debts?*
- *Have you planned a budget for retirement?*
- *Have you updated your estate plan?*
- *Have you reviewed your investments to match your risk assessment?*

16

LIVING IN RETIREMENT

You've made it! You're retired, and if you followed your plan, you'll be secure in knowing that you have enough funds to sustain you for the rest of your life.

At this point, communication with your children and family is more important than ever. As we age, we all will need help. Your family should know about your life plan and how to carry out your wishes if you need some assistance. As a matter of fact, they should have their own life plans and be living them. I know some families are uncomfortable with discussions about money, but those conversations should not be avoided.

If you cannot stand the idea that your children will know about all your assets, then at least you should let them know how to access information in case of emergency. I speak to thousands of retirees and always ask, "How many of you have given your cell phone password to your children in case anything were to happen?" Not a single person has ever raised their hand. Five or 10 years from now, records of everything we own will probably be able to be stored on a cell phone. If your children can't access your information or assets in the event something happens, it will be very difficult for them to help you.

Your plan isn't just for you and your retirement. It should provide reassurance to your family that everything will be okay if something were to happen to you. Though I have been in the financial industry since age 17, when I worked at a bank, it took my parents 15 years to open up to me about finances. They simply weren't ready to have that discussion. I'm fortunate my parents are still in great health, and I'm grateful that we've been able to plan for the future together.

SOCIAL SECURITY

Throughout our careers, most of us will contribute to social security. (Some public-sector employees may contribute to a different fund.) Depending on your expected expenses in retirement, social security can play a major role or a minimal one. Either way, you'll be able to use these funds. Based on how long you worked and how much you contributed, you could be looking at a monthly benefit of $3,000. This equates to $36,000 a year. If you have budgeted well and can live off expenses of $75,000, for example, social security will cover almost 50 percent of what you need!

The great thing about social security is its transparency. The agency has its own website where you can log in and track your benefit totals. I encourage everyone to visit the website. It's important to have this information when you hit a checkpoint and need to update your plan.

The current social security calculation is based on the age of full retirement. In 2019, this was 67 years old. You can begin taking social security as early as 62, but your benefit will be reduced. You can also put off taking your benefit past the age of 67. Each year you delay it beyond age 65, the more your benefit will increase. Everyone's decision is based on their individual situation. It should be part of your plan and a discussion with your advisor well before you get to retirement age.

I suggest following this easy rule: Take social security when you retire. If you retire before 62, take the benefit at 62. At the current rates, it will be about 30 percent less than your benefit at age 67, but you'll get five years of payments. If you work into your 60s, even part time, consider waiting until you need to replace the part-time income. Part of your decision should be based on your living longer than you expect. The longer you live, the more you'll appreciate having a larger payment.

CHARITABLE CONTRIBUTIONS

If you've already retired and have created enough income to not have to depend on your IRA funds, then consider another way to give to charity. Once you've reached the age of 72, your IRA is subject to a required minimum distribution (RMD)—a specified amount you are required to withdraw annually. Under the normal distribution process, if you don't need to live off the RMD, you can take it, pay the taxes, and give it to a charity of your choice. If your tax bracket is 25 percent and your RMD is $10,000, you'll pay taxes on $2,500 and have $7,500 to give. However, you can also set up your RMD to be distributed directly to the charity of your choice. A direct distribution is not taxed, so you'll end up gifting your portion plus what the IRS normally takes. Thus, your charity will receive the full $10,000.

LONG-TERM CARE

Long-term care (LTC) insurance has become more popular in the past decade, given skyrocketing health-care and medical costs. The costs for providing in-house care or paying for a nursing home can quickly outstrip a normal income, especially if special care or treatment is needed. Insurance options can help you hedge against these costs. The earlier you enroll, the cheaper the premium will be and the greater the benefit. However, the costs still add up over time. A pure LTC policy also is a gamble because you forfeit all the paid premiums if you never use it.

A newer option is a hybrid policy, such as an LTC policy attached to a life insurance policy, also known as an LTC rider. The idea is to add a death benefit to the LTC policy. In that case, if you don't need long-term care, your beneficiaries will receive an inheritance. However, the premiums and fees are higher on these types of policies. Also, the disclosures and calculations become more complex.

Even those of us in the industry have to reread these kinds of contracts multiple times to understand what they really mean. Providers of complex products hope that clients will trust them instead of doing the research. Don't let that happen to you. Once you are in an insurance product, you are committed. Research, research, and research all products before signing on the dotted line!

CHECKLIST

- Are you living within your budget?
- If not, have you considered a part-time job?
- Do you have a plan for social security?

- *Have you reviewed and updated your estate plan?*

- *Have you reviewed your tax planning for charitable contributions?*

- *Do you have a plan for covering health costs, including possible long-term care?*

- *Have you discussed your estate plan with your children or other loved ones?*

17

UNFORESEEN CIRCUMSTANCES

Remember our imaginary board game of Life? In that game, you might occasionally find yourself heading backward. In fact, certain events in our lives—unforeseen issues, problems, and setbacks—put a crimp in achieving our goals. Each of these circumstances are their own checkpoints and require that you review your plan to see if you are falling behind and whether you need to make some adjustments.

DIVORCE

Divorce can be the biggest hurdle in a life plan when it forces a change in your needs, wants, and dreams. If you're going through a divorce, you need to revisit every single item in your plan—budgeting, cash-flow analysis, retirement, and estate planning. If children are involved, review all the items on that checkpoint list as well. Be forewarned that this process may help your sanity, but your finances will still probably take a hit. There is an old joke: "Do you know why divorces are so expensive? Because they are worth it!" Regardless of how you feel about your new marital status, planning is crucial from this point forward.

Even if you assume that all assets will be split 50/50 between you and your spouse, most individuals retain an average of only 40 to 45 percent of assets due to legal fees and fees due to the liquidation of joint assets such as real estate. Moreover, the longer it takes to resolve the legal aspects of a divorce, the more expensive it becomes.

You need to rebalance your budget during and after a divorce. This is particularly important because you'll have to rebuild your income and monitor your spending, which may now include monthly payments for child support, alimony, and other agreed-upon expenses.

The next step is to create a new net worth balance sheet. On the plus side, the balance sheet should have all of your investment accounts and physical assets like your house. On the other side should be all of your debt, including your credit cards and mortgage. Your list of assets will look quite different after a divorce. Part of the planning process is to see where you are at this moment.

Then, you'll want to redo the rest of your financial plan by adjusting your assumptions and goals. It will be important to test your new plan to determine whether it is likely to work. Determine the new plan's probability of success by running it through simulations with your advisor. For instance, we use one called a Monte Carlo simulation to run thousands of scenarios and determine the probability of success. Finally, you'll need a new course of action to begin living your new plan.

LOSS OF A JOB

Anyone can lose a job in an instant. A company may downsize or fold, or you may be dismissed. You can't assume it will never happen.

You need to be prepared for a worst-case scenario. If you've been following your plan, emergency savings should be built up, and you'll have a back-up budget. Otherwise, now is the time to create a budget to act as a bridge until another job is found.

Remember your pillow test. If you lost your job today, could you sleep well tonight?

Look for ways to access lines of credit, just in case. It may sound counterintuitive to borrow in bad times, but emergencies are emergencies. We may hope that our unemployment is brief, but in certain industries, like oil and gas, layoffs can last a couple of years. For those who own homes, a home equity line of credit (HELOC) may be the answer. It allows you to pay debts other than a mortgage while you get your situation figured out. There is no cost to set it up, no cost to close it, and no prepayment penalties. You never have to borrow if you don't ever need it. It's there for emergencies. Another option is an asset-based line of credit against your investments. Or you may have a taxable account with investments that can have a line of credit attached to it. The latter is similar to a HELOC in that there's no cost to set it up, close it, or incur a prepayment penalty.

ILLNESS

It's difficult to think about a loved one suffering through a debilitating disease, but medical expenses can rack up to hundreds of thousands of dollars and sometimes millions. If you're lucky, you have solid health insurance coverage with a maximum out-of-pocket cost per year. Even so, the onset of illness can be a life-changing event that requires a checkpoint on your plan. You may find, for example, that your budget now has to account for new expenses for prescription medications or ongoing treatments.

It's important to review your health insurance. For young individuals, health savings account (HSA) plans can be attractive because you have the ability to build up an ongoing balance for health expenses. It carries forward year after year. However, it usually has a high deductible and high maximum out-of-pocket costs, making it less attractive later in life. If you're still working, review plans available to you through your employer.

Compare the low-deductible and low-maximum out-of-pocket options. Will you end up spending this much annually? If the answer is yes, sign up for the low-maximum out-of-pocket option. It will allow you to save money by not overspending each year.

A flexible spending account (FSA) can complement your health insurance. An FSA is similar to an HSA in how the funds are contributed. An FSA allows you to set an amount annually tax free to a separate account to be used for health expenses. The main difference is an HSA balance can accumulate, while an FSA has an annual spending requirement. One of an FSA's main benefits is that it can be used to cover the deductible amount for families who expect to max out their deductible. They receive a tax benefit for the FSA. In addition, the account is prepaid at the beginning of the period. For instance, if the amount you signed to contribute throughout the year to an FSA is $2,400, you'll start the year with $2,400 prepaid on your account. Remember the balance will disappear if you don't spend the FSA within a year.

The onset of an illness like Alzheimer's or dementia, which is more common among older individuals, calls for a review of your long-term care policy to see if the illness is covered. The reason for getting an LTC policy in the first place is to help with this type of cost.

Finally, review your estate plan to ensure it is up to date with current laws, in case the worst does happen. Also check to see if your estate is set up to cover your family's ongoing medical expenses if you die. If not, consider making this a priority in your plan.

CHILDREN

Yes, the arrival of children is a checkpoint—and a chapter—on its own. Including them here is important because they can derail the best of plans. Finding out you or your partner is pregnant can be emotionally and financially nerve-racking as you contemplate what lies ahead. Or you may be facing life as a single parent. Regardless of your marital status, it's important to sit down and create a life plan. Begin by drawing up a budget and figuring out your new expenses. Assess your cash flow and begin finding a way to establish an emergency fund.

It may also be more difficult to save money when you have a child. As parents, we tend to want to give our kids everything we didn't have and more. We want them to enjoy things they see on television or hear about from friends. Yet kids don't need or want every toy imaginable to be happy. I've seen that with my own daughters, who are showered with toys, clothes, and other goodies by their grandparents, aunts, and uncles.

I remember a Christmas when the girls opened toys that made my jaw drop because they were so expensive. However, my daughters were too busy making forts out of the wrapping and packaging to notice the extravagant contents. They played hide-and-seek in the forts all weekend. At that moment, I realized that sometimes we forget the important things in life are not the things we buy, but the love, laughs, and fun we share.

COLLEGE TUITION

No matter how much you plan, the high cost of college tuition can come as a shock. Please remember that you can get a loan for college, but you cannot take out a loan for retirement. Assisting your children with college should fall into the "wants" category. If you find—or fear—that you're falling behind in achieving the goals on your plan, remove college tuition from your budget. Once your finances get back on track, you can help your kids pay down any school loans.

YOU'VE FALLEN BEHIND

It's common to fall behind on retirement goals if you haven't been living your plan. If that happens, you may face some tough decisions: delay retirement, consider part-time work, or have a stay-at-home spouse take a job. While this may feel like a blow to your ego, there's no need to be discouraged. It's just another checkpoint that calls for your review. Delaying retirement a few years is not a big deal. Instead of retiring at age 62, your new goal becomes age 65. Remember that people today live longer than ever. There's a high probability that you or your spouse, if you have one, will still be around at 80.

Part-time work can help a lot in retirement. Find a job that you enjoy for 20 hours a week—something enjoyable that doesn't feel like work. Golf enthusiasts may relish working at a golf course, and DIYers may like being handy at a hardware or craft supplies store. Do you enjoy working with children? Perhaps helping at a school or library is for you. Working part time for a few years can improve the odds of having enough money for the rest of your life.

As for a stay-at-home mother or father taking a job, you may want to reevaluate your plan once kids are in school or moving out—especially if you're not meeting your goals. If the stay-at-home spouse can find a fulfilling job—part time, full time, or a hobby that pays—the extra income will improve your plan. Marriage is a team, and teammates help and support one another.

Depending on your age, social security can also supplement your income.

BANKRUPTCY

In the game of Monopoly, if you go bankrupt, you lose the game. In real life, however, bankruptcy may simply delay you from reaching your goals. During the financial crisis of 2008, for example, many people chose to go bankrupt because they bought houses they couldn't afford or borrowed too much and could not repay their debts.

Bankruptcy is a difficult decision to make. It stays on your record for seven years and may affect future loans or business decisions. If things go smoothly again, people eventually will lend to you, and your credit score will be repaired. It will cause you to lag behind where you planned to be, but the important point is that your game is not over. Plenty of successful individuals have gone through bankruptcy and bounced back. You can too.

DEATH OF A SPOUSE

It's excruciating to imagine life without a loved one. It may happen early in life or late, unexpectedly or after a long illness. The pain is real, and it's important to have a plan for this checkpoint. Not only can death be expensive, but it also impacts the lives of survivors in many ways.

I've been married for six years, and I have two beautiful daughters with another on the way. I find the thought of anyone dying traumatic, but I'm more concerned about my family's welfare without me. I'm the provider for my family and handle all of the finances. How would I carry them through a tragedy? How would my wife manage without me? The only way to maintain control is to have a plan with your family that accounts for financial matters. Beyond that, your spouse should understand the checkpoints, including budgets, cash flow, investments, and so on. Alternatively, the two of you should work with an advisor you both trust. It will help you to know the family is in good hands if anything happens.

CHECKLIST

- *Have you ensured that you have enough emergency savings?*

- *If any of these unfortunate events have occurred, have you reviewed and revised your budget, cash flow, investments, insurance, and tax and estate plans?*

18

UNEXPECTED BENEFITS

Planning for unforeseen circumstances is difficult, but it's critically important if you want to avoid having to completely redo your life plan. Remember, however, not all surprises are bad. Sometimes we're able to take advantage of unexpected benefits. Yes, they're rare and should never be assumed. But every so often, something comes along and gives us a boost to achieve our goals.

The most important of these benefits—and one we often forget about—is the power of time. The younger you are, the bigger your advantage in meeting your plan's goals or outperforming them. It's easy when we are in our 20s and 30s to put off saving for retirement or believe we can begin to budget after the kids are older. Don't give in to that mindset.

Time is all important. Take a look at the example that follows, which is based on a retiree with an annual income of $90,000. Social security will only make up 36 percent of what's needed to meet this person's life plan. You can see how much smaller monthly contributions are required for a retirement plan when 30 or 40 years are left until the big day. When only a decade remains before the big day, the contributions required are much greater.

Income Gap & Saving Shortfall

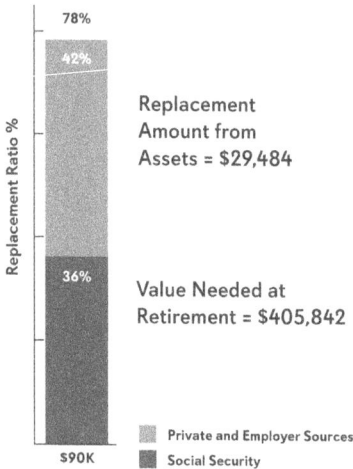

	Years of Savings	Monthly Contribution
	40	$203.79
	30	$404.02
	20	$878.37
	10	$2,476.47

Replacement Amount from Assets = $29,484

Value Needed at Retirement = $405,842

Private and Employer Sources
Social Security

78%
42%
36%
$90K

Replacement Ratio %

Based on a salary of $90,000 with a 78% replacement rate, assuming 30 years of contributions with a 6% annual return after fees and expenses. For illustration purposes only, **not guaranteed.** All investing involves risk.

INHERITANCE

Individuals hold a lot of different views about inheritance. Many people incorporate it into their plans as something they count on to achieve their goals, but that's a risky strategy. Far better to think of any inheritance as an unexpected gift. Build your plan without it. Any inheritance you receive acts like a slingshot to shoot you forward toward your goals.

Part of life planning is also legacy planning—both to you and from you—so it is important to discuss finances with your parents. I mentioned before that many parents haven't shared cell phone passwords, much less banking and investment account information, with their kids. The generations retiring today have parents who owned stocks directly with companies, possibly worth hundreds of thousands of dollars and spread among various transfer agents. Investors may have lost track of some of those accounts. I've heard stories of clients who inherited assets and took well over a year to locate everything. Even today, I meet with individuals who have accounts with more than five different custodians and wonder if they have captured everything. Helping them consolidate those investments and track down any loose ends is the first order of business.

Difficult as it may be, parents and grown children should share estate-plan details. What if one of your parents needed hospice care? Could your life plan handle an additional expense of $60,000 a year? Do you know if your parents have long-term care? Do they have assets to cover contingencies, or will it be up to you and your siblings, if you have any? Go ahead and schedule that tough Sunday-afternoon conversation. It will be worth it to you and your family.

CAREER PROGRESSION

If you have been carefully working on your life plan and living it since early in your career, you've likely earned promotions or opportunities that also brought raises and increased income. Career advancements allow you to put more of your earnings toward your goals—as long as you do not fall into the trap of more money, more expenses. That is how many Americans fall behind. The more they earn, the more they spend, and the more debt they accumulate. I've seen people with large incomes fail when they put their dreams before their needs.

Instead, why not let the increased income accumulate for a few years? Begin putting some of the money into a side account for a large purchase. Assign those dollars to a dream home, or invest it and let the earnings pay for your dreams.

Let's say you earned $60,000 early in your working life and created a plan for your needs based on that amount. A decade later, you earn $160,000 and still follow the plan with only modest adjustments to your budget. That additional income is now speeding you toward your goals and dreams.

OUTPACING YOUR PLAN

Let's imagine you've stayed on track, worked hard at your budget, and diligently reviewed your plan at every checkpoint, and suddenly you realize you've exceeded your needs, wants, and dreams. Congratulations! What a great feeling! But don't stop there or set new goals that can set you back later, such as a bigger home in retirement. Instead, think about something that currently stresses you out, and see if you can take it off your to-do list. Perhaps you can pay off your debt more quickly, retire earlier from a job you don't enjoy, or make a meaningful investment.

Aim to see how far beyond your plan you can go. Or evolve your plan to add new dreams important to you or your spouse. Did one of you cut back on something to make a goal more achievable? Add it back in, as long as you can keep moving forward.

CHECKLIST

- *Have you updated your wants and dreams to see if something is within reach?*

- *Have you reviewed and updated your tax plan to take advantage of any changes in the most efficient way?*

- *Have you revised your retirement plan to account for any additional benefits?*

19

ANNUAL CHECKPOINTS

Along with the major life events that constitute important checkpoints in your plan, you should designate one day a year to review the key elements emphasized in this book. It doesn't have to be January 1. Choose some date that's easy to remember, but be sure to go through the process each and every year.

As always, the first step is budgeting. If you spent more than you made this year, that needs to change. Don't delay the inevitable. Start with one paycheck. Can you go one paycheck without overspending? Increase it to a month. Then a quarter, six months, and eventually a year. Focusing on your budget will allow you to succeed in other areas of your plan.

The second is financial planning—cash flow, emergency savings, investments, and retirement planning. You don't need an in-depth review of everything. Just make sure you saved as much as you planned to save. It's also a good time to review the risk in your investments and make sure you are comfortable with it. The markets can move up or down 20 percent, which may affect the value of your assets. Talk with your advisor and make sure there's still a good probability that you can achieve your goals.

Retirement savings is part of financial planning, but it's still important to review separately once a year on its own. If your goal was to save $15,000 this year in your 401k and other funds, did you achieve it? If not, can you adjust your retirement plan to lower your expectations, add a year of employment, or make it up the following year?

Finally, make tax planning an end-of-year checkpoint. Do you need to increase contributions to your employer retirement plan or an IRA to offset taxes? Are you able to itemize this year?

CHANGES IN THE LAW

Legislative changes at the state or federal level may affect how much you can contribute to a 401k or an IRA. They may also alter estate plans, which people tend to create once on the assumption that laws won't change.

An out-of-date estate plan can defeat the entire purpose of having one and even put your assets at risk, especially in the case of a divorce. An advisor or attorney should create ad hoc checkpoints to review your estate plan in light of any changes to laws or your marital status.

Highlight these issues in your annual plan reviews, and ask your advisor to inform you if there is any important legislation to watch in the coming year. Will it impact your goals? How can you adjust your plan to capitalize on changes or mitigate risks?

> **CHECKLIST**

- ☑ *Have you set an annual date to review your whole plan?*
- ☑ *Do you have parts of the plan that are impacted by law changes?*

20

COMMON MISTAKES

An easy way to set yourself up for failure is by relying on false or wrong assumptions. Your plan will only be as good as the information you input. Do not assume you will get a 7 or 8 percent annual return on investments in your plan. If you do, great! That will allow you to achieve your goals more quickly. But it's far more realistic to use conservative return estimates—such as 4 percent when you're ready to take distributions. Four percent is achievable investing in lower-risk investments. I encourage you to plan for this while you're still in the years before retirement. A realistic plan that predicts you'll have enough funds for the rest of your life will give you tremendous confidence.

RETIREMENT CALCULATORS

Defaults that are preset on retirement calculators can be misleading. It's important to understand how they work. These calculators automatically compute retirement figures based on your starting principal, how much you will save and invest annually, how much time until you retire, and your expected rate of return. Assumptions are built into these calculators as defaults that can lead clients into believing they will be fine by retirement. If individuals depend solely on these calculators, however, they may be surprised in 20 years when they find out the numbers were wrong.

Some of these assumptions include an annual rate of return for investments that may be as high as 10 percent. It takes a lot of risk to achieve that rate of return in today's market. That isn't the only problem. Typically, the calculators don't account for inflation. They assume that an investor is aiming to have $1 million in 20 years, but $1 million today is not $1 million two decades from now. The target rate of inflation for the Federal Reserve is 2 percent, so the equivalent of $1 million today would be $1,485,000 in 20 years. That should be your target.

One of the elements accounting for an inflation rate of 2 percent is health care, but health-care costs have risen much more quickly than normal inflation. You should look at costs such as health care and assume a higher rate of increase when calculating retirement. I like to use a rate of 5.5 percent.

All these assumptions can have a huge impact on whether someone will achieve their goals, especially when it comes to the rate of return. Even though the stock market has had roughly an annual 8 percent return over the past 100 years, most investments do not equal that. For one thing, most investors do not take as much risk as the whole market. There is always the chance that the market will not perform as well in the future as it has the past century. Far better to assume that your investments will not earn that much.

As an example, let's say someone new to the workforce hopes to work for 30 years and decides their goal is to invest $10,000 every year. A standard retirement calculator, based on an 8 percent return, computes an end total of $1,223,000. Realistically, though, if they earn only 5 percent annually, the total is just $697,700. Relying on the calculator alone could lead to a large shortfall in their plan.

THE IMPACT OF FEES

For every investment, there is some type of fee. It may be levied for managing assets or be paid in the form of commissions for trading. If you want to invest for retirement, it will be nearly impossible to avoid any fees. The goal, however, is to understand how they are calculated and how to get the best return on investment (ROI), after fees.

For example, if I ask clients if they want to pay .25 percent or .5 percent in fees, they will undoubtedly choose the former. But if I say the first investment returns 3 percent annually and the second returns 6 percent, they will choose the latter, as it has a better ROI. Generally, once your fees get to the 2 percent or higher mark, it becomes very hard to consistently make a profit, especially if the investment is flat or down for a year.

Most investors understand fees can eat into their investment. The difficulty is finding and understanding them to determine if you are in the right investments for you. Look for fees in common products that are marked as investment management fees, mortality and expense fees in annuities, administration fees, technology expenses, and billings per hour. You can also check the expense ratios of investments at Morningstar.com, which is a website that analyzes all mutual funds and exchange-traded funds (ETFs).

UNREALISTIC EXPECTATIONS

We tend to assume that our income will rise over time, along with inflation. If that happens, great! But it's not always the case. Our income may remain unchanged, or we may be demoted or have to take a lower-paying position. Build a plan around what you currently make. Do not assume that you will earn more money as you get older, but if you do earn more, you will have outperformed your goals.

FOCUSING ON PERFORMANCE

When it comes to money management, focusing on performance can create bad habits. Too often clients hear that something can earn a guaranteed 8 percent on an investment. So, they make changes in their portfolio to obtain it. Then, within six months, their portfolio is down 15 percent. Your plan should include a personalized portfolio, especially as your wealth grows and your assets become more complex.

Performance will always go up and down. Rather than focusing solely on a possibly unrealistic return, build your plan with the idea of stress-testing performance—making sure you will still be successful in a worst-case scenario. When you do that, an exceptionally good return just helps you to achieve your goals more quickly and easily.

DON'T TRY TO GO IT ALONE, AND ALWAYS KEEP GOING

Creating and adapting a successful plan takes a team effort, and a majority of people will need some help. A spouse or family member may be your first teammate. They need to know your goals and your plan. They can remind you what you set out to do if you get off track. It's easy to be caught up in the heat of the moment or led astray by a busy week. A note of caution: Once you forget what you need to do to stick to a budget, your goals will fall by the wayside. Before you know it, you'll have booked six trips or purchased a new car.

If you and your spouse find it difficult to live your plan, work with an advisor who will tell you what you need to hear and challenge your assumptions. Think of your family doctor: Unless you went to medical school, you need a competent physician to help keep you healthy and to care for you when you are not. As you get older and have a family, a physician relationship becomes even more important. For financial matters, an advisor can play a similar role.

Putting a plan on autopilot is another common mistake. Many individuals go through the process of creating a plan, then never look at it again. It sits on a shelf instead of providing a useful guide for the rest of your life. Either you forget about it or it comes up only in meetings with your advisor. Ineffective advisors may not even let you know if you are on track with your goals. They assume you're a happy client, responsible for your own plan. You should know it, right? Wrong! Your advisor should be asking probing questions to see if you've arrived at any of the checkpoints we've covered in this book. If you have, it calls for a review focused on that checkpoint.

Every year, you and your advisor should measure how you did, what changed in your life, and how you should plan for the next year. Still, as my dad used to say, "If you want to make God laugh, make a plan." Things will happen, and you'll need to adjust. That's life. Recognizing the change and adapting your plan is what will make you successful.

CHECKLIST

- ✓ Do you understand how your plan works?
- ✓ Is it up to date?
- ✓ Do you review your assumptions annually?

21

HOW TO CHOOSE A LIFE PLANNER

A man walks down a street and comes across two gates. Inside the one on the left, he sees people holding hands and singing in sweet harmony. Inside the gate on the right, he sees what looks like an awesome party, with people swimming in a pool, playing, and laughing. The guard at the left gate says that the gentleman is welcome and will be safe inside. The guard on the right promises that every day will be a party if the gentleman comes inside.

The man chooses the gate on the right and enters, and after a few minutes, everything disappears in flames.

"Where did the party go?" he asks the gatekeeper.

"When you were outside the gate, you were a prospect," the guard says. "Now you're a client.'"

Unfortunately, this story shows the attitude of some firms in our industry—the ones who are focused on growing their sales instead of building and servicing their relationships. My purpose is not to bash the financial advisor community. After all, I'm a financial advisor myself. One of my goals is to change the negative perception of financial advisors, most of whom are qualified and trustworthy, while teaching investors how to take control of their lives and develop action plans they can live with.

I like to use the analogy of a home purchase. Many firms act like developers who plan communities with fixed designs and their own idea of how many bedrooms and bathrooms are needed. You may buy a house that fits into their scheme or purchase one that has already been built. However, when you walk into the house, it doesn't feel right. The house doesn't flow the way you wanted. You like some fixtures or finishes and dislike others. But it's too late; the house is built, and changes will be costly.

Ideally, a developer should build that home in partnership with you, working with your preferences and adjusting them as needed. Similarly, a financial advisor should customize a plan to your needs and wants instead of offering you a cookie-cutter solution.

Many jobs use the term "financial advisor," but you want someone who is licensed and acts as a fiduciary. A financial advisor needs to have at least a Series 65 or 66 license to qualify as an investment advisor representative. If you are considering hiring someone, you can check on their license status at https://brokercheck.finra.org. If they are not listed, then they may not be qualified to be your advisor.

A great advisor should help a client with all aspects of their planning—from budgeting and estate work to tax planning—even if it is not included in their compensation. They should help your family succeed. Find an advisor you can get to know, like, and trust. Your relationship should allow you the comfort of not having to monitor your investments daily.

There is a key difference between an investment manager and life planner. An investment manager manages portfolios, which may be restricted to those of his or her firm or a wider variety. A life planner has access to hundreds of money managers and other forms of investment management for a client and can help a client invest the way they want or need to. The goal isn't to outperform the market year after year. It's to help you outperform your goals and to advise you on every aspect of your life that involves money. If your goal is retirement, their goal should be to help you achieve that comfortably.

Consider the way an advisor treats you. Do you feel important? If the advisor is with a firm, how much turnover takes place in terms of staff and clients? How long has the firm been around? Are they profitable and likely to remain in business?

Review how the advisor invests assets. Can he or she customize a portfolio to your situation, or is every client limited to certain models?

Look for a firm with a low turnover of advisors and a high client-retention ratio, which can indicate a healthy company culture. Ask how long the advisors have been there. Is the firm growing, or is it a one-advisor shop? A small firm can be attractive since it can focus its attention on you.

If your advisor is close to retirement age, ask about their own retirement plan and about a succession plan in case anything happens to them. Who will work with you and continue to ensure your success? The average age of an advisor is 55 years old. If you are 65 and your advisor is 65, the advisor is likely to retire soon. Who will be checking on your life plan in 10 years, especially if the firm is small?

If the firm is large, ask about the advisor-to-client ratio. A good rule of thumb is to have no more than 100 households per advisor. That number assures that investors receive enough attention. If senior advisors have junior staff members working with them, the ratio may exceed 1 to 100 and still work. However, if the firm is merely soliciting new clients and using a call center to service them, that can't compare to having a legitimate working relationship with an advisor.

Finally, be clear about what you want from an advisor. Make a list of your priorities, then try and narrow it to the most important three or five items. Certainly, you want someone who understands finance and investment, among other issues with which you may not be familiar. You may also want an advisor who can invest funds wisely and make logical choices with your specific goals in mind. Make sure you find an advisor who will fulfill these goals. Then make sure they actually do.

CHECKLIST

- ☑ *Does your advisor work under the fiduciary rule as a registered investment advisor?*
- ☑ *Is your advisor compensated to earn and keep your business?*
- ☑ *Is there a fee or sales charges to start or end the relationship?*
- ☑ *Can your advisor customize a plan for your situation?*
- ☑ *Does your advisor's actions match his or her words?*

Conclusion

LIVE YOUR PLAN!

I wrote this book to inspire everyone not only to get a plan, regardless of age or stage of life, but also to *live* one. My goal is to demonstrate how a plan should be active (checked and adapted) at key moments in your life. If you have a plan but it sits on a shelf and you are not actively working with it, it's not a plan. It's a history book collecting dust.

We in the financial industry still have a lot of work to do to earn your trust. However, do not let that hold you back from seeking assistance if you need it. Great advisors exist out there who can help you plan your future and exceed your goals. The good thing about the current industry is the flexibility of investments and the existence of fee-only advisors. You can start a relationship with an advisor for no cost, and you can end it with no additional cost. You are not locked in to a relationship for a set period of time.

These advisor-client relationships are worth cultivating, since this type of advisor has to continuously earn your trust. And if you're working with a financial organization, I hope it is proactive and constantly ensuring that you are on track with your plan throughout your life.

Perhaps the most important takeaway is that a plan should evolve and adapt. There's no pass/fail option. Your plan is a guide to help you achieve your life goals, which can and will change. You need to monitor it. You may fall behind or creep ahead, but that doesn't mean it will fail or collapse. All these setbacks do is encourage us to include contingencies in our plan. If you are unsure how to do this, turn to an advisor whose job is to encourage you to achieve your plan and help you evolve it along the way. You should never struggle alone to reach your needs, wants, and dreams.

ACKNOWLEDGMENTS

I want to thank my parents for inspiring me to write this book. They were my first teachers of finance and my first mentors. Their patience and humility through the process of writing this book and throughout my life helped me get where I am today.

To my wife of six years, for being my best friend and unselfishly supporting me as I worked and wrote this book, and for leading the charge with our three children while I did so. She never complained about the travel or long nights as she captained our family team. In addition, thank you to my wife's family for all the help and the influence each of you have had on our daughters and myself.

To the best three daughters a dad has ever had: Layla, Phoenix, and Zuri. Thank you for inspiring me every day to be the best dad possible and always making sure I come home to hugs, no matter how my day was.

Thank you to the mentors I have had that have influenced my ethics and the way I treat people. It is important to have leaders who guide you along the right path, and I appreciate you allowing me to learn through your experiences.

I want to thank TCG and the team there, which includes our clients. Everyone at TCG has influenced me in some way, and the family-first attitude has been an enormous influence in my personal life. When I had my third daughter, it was the team at TCG and my clients that encouraged me to take time off and enjoy the moment.

It was you who made me realize that the memories we make with our loved ones and friends are what create our personal wealth.

Finally, I want to express my appreciation to our clients who took a chance on me. The hardest decision in the world is trusting someone else with your money. I am honored that so many chose to trust me with their finances, future, and legacy. Our clients help our company grow and evolve so that we can help more people. Thank you from the bottom of my heart.

ABOUT THE AUTHOR

DENNIS BIELIK is a managing director of TCG Advisors, where he's on a mission to help individuals of all ages and wealth make better financial decisions. He is an industry expert, speaker, and advisor with over 10 years of experience in finance

In 2019, Dennis was named as one of the *Financial Times* top 401 advisors, a list of the top retirement advisors nationwide, and his firm has been recognized as a top registered investment advisor in the country by publications like *Financial Times*. He was also named as a Forbes Best-in-State Wealth Advisor for Texas in 2020.

Dennis is passionate about helping as many people as possible be successful in their financial planning. He firmly believes everyone should have a plan and be able to live a plan with help if they need it. He hopes to share his experience and success to influence young financial planners to help their clients better.

He started in banking in 2005 with Woodforest National Bank. Since then, he has held various positions and leadership roles at financial firms like Charles Schwab, Scottrade, and TD Ameritrade.

He has two bachelor of arts degrees and a master's degree from the University of Texas at Arlington. Dennis is a CFA Charter holder, CFP Charter holder, and FRM Charter holder. He is a member of the CFA society, Global Association of Risk professionals, and Association of Corporate Growth. He lives in Austin with his wife and three daughters.

NOTES

NOTES

NOTES

NOTES

NOTES

NOTES

NOTES

NOTES